DOING BUSINESS IN HUNGARY

The Confederation of British Industry (CBI) is the voice of British business and is committed to alerting British companies to the commercial potential of Central and Eastern Europe. Its Initiative Central and Eastern Europe provides pragmatic and detailed advice on how to develop business and operate successfully in these emerging market economies.

The CBI also organises trade missions to the countries in the region and provides a forum in which to meet senior policy makers and business executives. Further details of all the CBI's Central and Eastern European activities are available from its head-quarters.

CBI
Centre Point
103 New Oxford Street
London WC1A 1DU
Tel: 071–379–7400

CBI

*Initiative Central
& Eastern Europe*

DOING BUSINESS IN

HUNGARY

SECOND EDITION

CREDITANSTALT
KPMG PEAT MARWICK • S J BERWIN & CO
SAATCHI & SAATCHI • G J W • ETD
BRITISH CHAMBER OF COMMERCE IN HUNGARY

KOGAN
PAGE

This book is written on the basis of information
constant in (September) 1993.

First published in 1991
Reprinted 1991
Second edition 1994

Kogan Page Limited
120 Pentonville Road
London N1 9JN

© Confederation of British Industry, 1991, 1994

British Library Cataloguing in Publication Data

A CIP record for this book is available from the British Library.

ISBN 0 7494 1176 7

Typeset by Photoprint, Torquay, Devon
Printed in England by Clays Ltd, St Ives plc

Contents

PART I: THE BUSINESS CONTEXT

PART II: THE BUSINESS INFRASTRUCTURE

PART III: THE OPTIONS FOR WESTERN BUSINESS

PART IV: CASE STUDIES

APPENDICES

The Contributors

Creditanstalt, a universal bank with 30,000 shareholders worldwide, is the most internationally oriented institution among the Austrian banks. Since 1990, Creditanstalt has put special emphasis on building up an operative network in the reforming countries of Central and Eastern Europe. By now commercial banking subsidiaries have been established in Hungary, Poland, the Czech Republic and Slovenia, and one is planned to be opened in Slovakia in the middle of 1994. By 1995 Creditanstalt's commercial banking network in those countries will comprise 25 units. An additional focal point is investment banking, complemented by leasing and trading activities.

KPMG Peat Marwick is the UK member firm of KPMG, one of the largest international firms of accountants, tax advisers and management consultants. The Hungarian member firm, KPMG Reviconsult, was established as an independent accountancy and consultancy practice in Budapest in 1989. As well as providing a full range of professional services to its Hungarian clients and to international clients with investments in Hungary, KPMG is also actively involved in assisting in the state privatisation programme.

SJ Berwin & Co is a City law firm specialising in corporate finance, banking, tax, commercial property, international and EEC law, commercial litigation and commercial property. From the firm's inception, its partners have advised in commercial transactions in Eastern European countries and are in continuous contact with ministers and senior officials in government and managers of corporate entities and have also developed close working relationships with commercial lawyers in those jurisdictions.

Saatchi & Saatchi Advertising Worldwide is one of the world's leading advertising and communications networks with 143 offices in 77 countries. Saatchi & Saatchi Advertising established its first office in Budapest in April 1990, closely followed by Warsaw and Prague. Today, they have the leading advertising agency network in the region with offices in Bucharest, Sofia, Ljubljana, Moscow, St Petersburg and Zagreb. Representation is planned in 1994 in Tirana and Skopje.

GJW Government Relations is the specialist political consultancy and lobbying firm providing a comprehensive service on all matters relating to government and political relations across the whole of Central and Eastern Europe and Russia. Its office in Hungary, opened in 1990, provides a full range of professional services to international as well as Hungarian clients. GJW also has offices in Prague, Warsaw, Bucharest, Sofia and Moscow, in addition to London and Brussels.

ETD Ltd and its founders were the pioneering investment, mergers and acquisitions specialists in Hungary with a permanent residence for 30 years. They have established more foreign investors in Hungary than any other company or bank.

The British Chamber of Commerce in Hungary has been in operation for over two and a half years to provide a forum for members to meet and exchange views on a regular basis; to represent their interests to the Hungarian authorities; to provide members with up-to-date information on various matters and help their activities by providing various services. It also offers various business services to non-members. The Chamber now has 125 members.

Foreword

The CBI's intention to inform decision makers and the business community in Britain and the developed world about the economic conditions and prospects in Hungary is highly appreciated both by the Hungarian government and the rapidly emerging entrepreneurial community. It is especially valuable as Hungarian–British relations date back so long. In 1993 Hungarian exports were worth US$200 million and imports US$300 million. The United Kingdom was Hungary's eighth largest foreign trading partner.

The first edition of *Doing Business in Hungary* was published in 1991. In its Foreword the first freely elected Prime Minister of Hungary since World War II, the late Dr József Antall, outlined the most important tasks of the new government: to establish the institutional framework for a market economy; to obtain majority private ownership by way of privatisation; to safeguard entrepreneurs; and to modernise the banking system as an incentive for domestic and foreign investment.

Three-and-a-half years on the Hungarian government is proud to announce progress. The legal and institutional frameworks are in place and working in Hungary; parliament has enacted approximately 400 new laws; exports and imports are liberalised; and the private sector generates 50 per cent of GDP. Nevertheless, it must be reported that economic indicators are below expectations.

Hungary aims to rapidly develop its infrastructure and telecommunications. As a result of association and free trade agreements with the EC, EFTA and CEFTA countries, 80 per cent of Hungary's export products have more secure access to Europe – a market of 400 million consumers. All these steps strengthen Hungary's position as part and partner of a greater Europe. The international sector is larger in Hungary than in any other former Comecon country.

At the end of 1993 foreign direct investment in Hungary stood at US$7 billion, representing more than half of all investments in Eastern-Central Europe. A record number of joint ventures and 100 per cent foreign-owned firms (19,000 in total) have been established. The market maturity of Hungary is also reflected in the 1200 joint ventures set up by Hungarian entrepreneurs in neighbouring countries.

British companies are strongly involved in the Hungarian economy – their investment amounts to over US$400 million. They are represented in (*inter alia*) the canning, confectionery, tobacco and motor vehicle industries. There are more than 350 companies with British participation, including McVitie's, BAT, Shell, Marks & Spencer and David Brown. Their presence is evidence of the successful measures and incentives put in place by the Hungarian government. It also reflects the confidence of the British business community in the new democratic Hungary.

Due to its excellent geographical location, Hungary aims to become Eastern-Central Europe's corporate and financial head-quarters. Banks, financial institutions and trading houses are all welcome in a politically stable Hungary.

Professor Dr Béla Kádár DSc
Minister of International Economic Relations, Hungary
February, 1994

Preface

Political stability and steady economic policies have marked Hungary's progress towards a free market since 1990. In an increasingly turbulent region, the continuity provided by the government of Joszef Antall, Hungary's Prime Minister from 1990 until his death at the end of 1993, appears more and more impressive. Whatever the elections may bring in the spring of 1994, the principles of a free market and a pluralist democracy are now firmly established.

This is a second edition of a book originally published in the summer of 1991. Much has happened since then: reform policies are being carried through and a wealth of operating experience has been accumulated. This new edition is designed to provide international companies with a commentary on the market's political and economic context, to assess the development of a commercial framework conforming to the needs of international companies and to review the options for developing business in the market.

The CBI is grateful to the principal contributors to this book: Creditanstalt, a leading Austrian bank firmly established in Hungary; KPMG Peat Marwick, a major international accountancy practice with a significant local presence; and SJ Berwin & Co, a leading British law firm.

Supporting chapters have been written on: marketing by the local office of Saatchi & Saatchi; the potential of the country and its people by ETD Ltd, one of the most experienced specialist investment advisors in the market; and politics and trade relations by GJW, one of the first government relations firms established in Hungary. Peter Tarnoy, Tibor Vidos, Karoly Fekete and Calum Chace all made valuable contributions.

A review of opportunities by sector has been provided by the British Chamber of Commerce in Hungary, set up in 1991 and now going from strength to strength. The CBI is grateful as well to the

European Bank for Reconstruction and Development, the World Bank, the EC's PHARE programme, the UK's Know How Fund and the British Embassy in Budapest for the information they supplied.

Four case studies in Part IV cover the strategic attractions of the Hungarian market and how early aspirations worked out in practice. McVitie's has purchased one of Hungary's premier biscuit producers and has introduced one of its international brands of crisps to the market. Watmoughs has bought a printing plant on the outskirts of Budapest with a view to meeting the demands of international publishers, as well as capturing orders for a new phenomenon in Hungary, company annual reports. Coats Vyella has bought back its holding in a mill confiscated by the communists at the end of the 1940s and is supplying thread to local companies, who are producing clothes for some of the biggest names in international design. Finally, Hungary's genius for mathematics was put to practical effect by Robert Stein of Andromeda in creating a major force in software for computer games.

The CBI thanks all those that have played a part in putting together this book. I hope it will provide international companies with the guidance and information they need to develop business successfully in one of the most dynamic markets in central Europe. There is an extensive list of contacts in the last appendix for those with questions still to ask.

Alan J Lewis CBE
Chairman, CBI Initiative Central and Eastern Europe
February 1994

Part I

The Business Context

1

Economic Reform

Creditanstalt-Bankverein

Hungary's adjustment-induced crisis during the three years from 1990 to 1992 has ended. However, contrary to expectations that the current stagnation would be followed by an upswing in 1993, it seems increasingly likely that the take-off may be delayed for three main reasons: exports to the West as a vital source of growth suffered a setback in early-1993; secondly, domestic demand has so far failed to pick up at the expected rate; and thirdly, unemployment is still high and the budget deficit remains an urgent problem. All these factors suggest that Hungary may have to wait another year before economic growth resumes.

Hungary's most impressive successes so far have been achieved in the monetary sphere and in foreign trade. These include falling inflation rates, rising exports to Western countries, a balanced current account and vigorously expanding monetary reserves (primarily the result of a surge in foreign direct investment and an unchanged level of foreign debt). The inflow of foreign capital indicates that Hungary's economic reforms enjoy a high level of credibility abroad. At the end of 1992 Hungary held the investment record among the Central and East European reforming countries. Of total foreign direct investment in this region, 55 per cent (US$4.7 billion) went to Hungary. Since 1990, Hungary has attracted some US$1.5 billion annually.

BACKGROUND TO THE REFORMS

Hungary has a long-standing tradition of gradual but steady progress in reform. As early as 1968 it started to make efforts to adapt central planning in a more market-oriented direction. The 'New Economic Mechanism' (NEM), adopted on 1 January 1968, was a reform model. Its most important characteristic was the elimination of centralised directives and commands. Furthermore, the NEM envisaged a closer direct relationship between the domestic economy and foreign markets.

This reform policy suffered a set-back in the period 1973–78. The tougher policy pursued after the 'Spring of Prague' had been suppressed and led to recentralisation accompanied by a wave of industrial concentration. Obviously, however, the Hungarian economy was unable to carry out the necessary structural changes under these centralist conditions. This was reflected in the growing foreign trade deficits, leading to a sharp increase in foreign debt.

In the period 1979–83 the NEM approach was partly reintroduced as a means of restoring the external trade equilibrium. In 1981 the 'branch ministries' which had remained the main vehicle of state control and planning were merged into a single Ministry of Industry with reduced powers. However, to maintain the country's liquidity position, import restrictions had to be implemented in mid-1982, and temporarily (until 1984) recourse was sought to centralist methods of administrative control. As a result, companies' independence was again reduced.

The third reform period (1984–87) was marked by renewed attempts to carry out extensive economic reforms. The economic difficulties which Hungary faced at the end of 1983 were due, according to the advocates of the reforms, above all to the inconsistent application and execution of the NEM. During this period, state enterprises were emancipated from ministerial and from party control – most enterprises were given a 'self-governing statute'. Closely connected with this step, price-setting was liberalised so that prices could at least partially reflect 'costs'. Furthermore, the number of enterprises licensed to conduct foreign trade was increased substantially.

In Hungary, as well as in the West, there was uncertainty concerning the reaction of the USSR. But when the 'new economic strategy' proposed by Gorbachev in April 1985 was adopted at the 27th Party Congress of the Communist Party of the Soviet Union (in March 1986), this finally paved the way for Hungary to implement far-reaching reforms. Special mention should be made of three laws which had a particularly strong effect on the economic and social system.

1. The Bankruptcy Law, which came into force on 1 September 1986, put an end to the era of absolute job security.

2. The banking legislation dismantled the classic monobank system, changing it to a two-tier system with commercial banks and a National Bank without commercial bank functions.

3. The new Tax Law was prepared in 1987 and came into force on 1 January 1988. In addition to introducing a personal income tax for the first time, the tax law provided for the introduction of value added tax (VAT) and the profit tax system.

From reform to a new system (1988–89)

In 1988 the reform process accelerated considerably. An ambitious import liberalisation programme was combined with (and this is one of the focal points) liberalisation of prices, to achieve competition on the domestic market (50 per cent of consumer prices were deregulated). The Foreign Investment Act (1988, with subsequent amendments) provided for the protection of foreign investments, the repatriation of profits and compensation in case of expropriation.

Another decisive change compared with the old centrally planned economic system was the Companies Act (1989). For the first time since the introduction of the communist regime, private persons were granted the same rights as the state to establish or participate in business activities. This allowed the creation of small to medium-sized enterprises (up to 500 employees) in almost all sectors of the economy.

Finally, in 1989, the system was changed completely when the power monopoly of the Communist Party was broken. The transition from a party-state – where actual power is exercised by a group of persons (the political party) – to a state under the rule of law, in which the public authorities are subject to laws that can be enforced before independent courts, manifested itself by the establishment of independent administrative and constitutional courts. As a result of the collapse of the central planning authorities, business enterprises had to be defined by law – ie to provide them with a legal framework. The Transformation Act (1989) enabled production units to be transformed into joint stock or limited liability companies. With the foundation of the

State Property Agency (1990), the re-establishment of the stock exchange (1990) and – most importantly – the introduction of accounting laws (1991), the main institutional and legal pre-conditions for a market economy have been met.

The 'programme of conversion and development' approved by Parliament in March 1991, realistically recognised that the new legal and institutional framework of a social market economy was not going to be immediately operational. However, the corner-stones are set and a process of fine tuning has to follow, most probably via a process of trial and error.

ECONOMIC POLICY IN 1992–93

Inflationary pressures are part of the transition costs that Hungary has to bear. The move towards a market economy encompassing price liberalisation, the removal of subsidies, the dismantling of Comecon and its effects on the terms of trade, and the depreciation of the forint have pushed the inflation rate upwards. In its short-term stabilisation strategy, the Hungarian government has relied on a policy mix of restrictive budgetary, monetary and income policies in order to keep inflation under control.

In 1992, economic policy was aimed at slowing inflation in the wake of the devaluation of the forint and the liberalisation of prices. The budget deficit was to be reduced from 4.5 per cent of GDP to 1.5 per cent and domestic credit was to decline by nearly 10 per cent in real terms. Exchange rate policy was geared towards slowing the nominal depreciation of the forint so as to encourage employers to check wage increases. At the same time, new laws governing domestic banks and corporate bankruptcies were intended to tighten financial discipline over the majority of companies not yet privatised. In particular, the Banking Law required banks to make provisions against non-performing assets while raising capital to comply with the capital adequacy guidelines of the Bank for International Settlements.

Inflation during this period appeared to be under control, as the average annual increase in consumer prices was reduced from 35 per cent in 1991 to 23 per cent in 1992. However, the fiscal consequences of bank restructuring and corporate bank-ruptcies were more severe than intended. Bank and dividend payments fell sharply as unemployment payments rose, and the fiscal deficit reached 7 per cent of GDP. Banks largely ceased lending to borrowers other than the government.

Economic policies in 1993 target reducing the fiscal deficit to about 6 per cent of GDP and further reducing domestic credit in real terms. Monetary policy, however, is likely to focus on further reductions in interest rates, which were cut sharply in 1992. A credit consolidation scheme has been initiated to remove bad debts from the banks' balance sheets to enable them to begin lending again and to allow privatisation of the major banks to begin later this year. Exchange rate policy tries to prevent further losses in competitiveness after a marked real appreciation in 1992. Structural policies enlarge the scope of preferential schemes for domestic investors in privatisations.

Fiscal policy

Despite government intentions to the contrary, the budgetary position has deteriorated substantially over the past few years. The ratio of the consolidated central government deficit to GDP widened by more than 7 percentage points between 1989 and 1992. Real GDP fell by 18 per cent in the same period, which rapidly eroded the tax base and added to expenditure pressures.

In mid-1993 the Hungarian parliament approved a supplementary budget for 1993 and an austerity package that meets International Monetary Fund demands to reduce the state deficit and paves the way for a US$600 million IMF standby credit. It is intended that the austerity package will bring the budget deficit down to 5.6 per cent of GDP. On the revenue side, the revisions include tax increases, among them the raising of the lower VAT rate from 6 per cent to 10 per cent. On the expenditure side, the government intends to cut costs by slashing subsidies to certain state sectors (such as the arms industry) that are being phased out. From a structural point of view, state expenditures are intended increasingly to promote overall economic growth.

Exchange rate policy

At present the Hungarian forint is *de facto* fully convertible for current account transactions by resident enterprises, banks and foreign joint ventures (repatriation of profits). The government has tried to use the exchange rate to both curb inflation and regulate the current account. Over the past three years the forint has been devalued by less than the rate of inflation, which has led the forint to appreciate in real effective terms. In response to the unexpected weakness of exports in late-1992 and early-1993, the emphasis of exchange rate policy has shifted in 1993. Higher and more frequent devaluations in recent months could be a sign of more expansionary policy shifts to come.

Monetary policy

As a result of very tight monetary policy, nominal interest rates are currently still quite high, around 25–30 per cent, although they have fallen from a mid-1992 peak of about 45 per cent as inflation has gradually declined. Real growth in the money supply has been insignificant or negative over the past three years. The National Bank of Hungary expects that broad money will grow by 22–26 per cent in 1993, exceeding growth in nominal GDP and probably also inflation. As a result of a less restrictive monetary policy, strong downward pressure on interest rates has already begun. The National Bank of Hungary started to reduce its base rate in October 1992 – the first cut in two years – and further reductions followed in 1993. Similarly, the National Savings Bank and the other commercial banks cut many of their interest rates in early-1993.

Structural reform

Significant efforts were made in the recent past to strengthen the economy's institutional framework. The new Bankruptcy Law, which became effective on 1 January 1992, forced debtor companies to file for bankruptcy if they held obligations that had been overdue for more than 90 days. As a consequence the number of bankruptcies and liquidations exploded in 1992. This contributed to the increase in unemployment, as companies shed labour to survive. While the law served its original purpose of weeding out a large number of bankrupt companies, it has also taken many fundamentally sound companies down with them. The government has therefore decided to amend the law in 1993 in order to relax the automatic triggering mechanism and to make it easier for potentially viable bankrupt enterprises to escape liquidation.

The financial difficulties of the business sector have had a severe impact on banks. This impact coincided with the introduction of more stringent accounting and loan classification rules stipulated by the new Banking Law. The banks were provisioning heavily against bad and doubtful debt during the course of 1992, attempting to meet the capital/asset ratio of 8 per cent required by law. At the end of 1992 a credit consolidation scheme was instituted to manage the bad debts of the main commercial banks. Undercapitalised banks were allowed to swap loans classified as bad in 1991 and 1992 for 20-year state bonds in an amount equal to 100 per cent and 50 per cent, respectively, of face value.

Privatisation

With progress on privatisation remaining rather disappointing, the government started to speed up the programme and give greater preference to Hungarian buyers through mass privatisation. Privatisation of state-owned enterprises, managed by the State Property Agency (SPA) has been slower than originally intended. Rough estimates indicate that about 18 per cent of 'business property' held by the state in 1990 had been privatised by the end of 1992, as compared with an original target of transferring 50 per cent of state-owned assets to private ownership by the end of 1994.

The prevailing form of privatisation has been the direct sale of majority stakes in companies to foreign industrial investors, who have thus gained management and financial control. According to SPA, both in 1991 and 1992 nearly two-thirds of privatisation income came from foreign sources. In this way Hungarian enterprises gain access to modern management skills, additional finance for investment projects and new markets. This year the privatisation process is to be accelerated by the recently established State Assets Handling Company (SAC). This organisation is now responsible for the management of state-owned companies, so SPA will be able to concentrate exclusively on privatisation activities.

To speed up the privatisation process and to make privatisation more domestically sustained, the government is now attempting to attract domestic investors. New ways of privatisation are management buyouts and the 'Employee Partial Ownership Programme'. The latter scheme means that at least half of the employees unite to found a company to buy their enterprise. For this purpose they can obtain a so-called 'existence loan'. Similarly, a government decree has recently further eased the credit conditions of the share programme, while 'privatisation leasing' is a newly introduced method enabling entrepreneurs to acquire management control of those small and medium-sized companies that were tendered for but for which no bids were accepted.

In a major policy shift towards mass privatisation, the authorities have decided to introduce voucher-like credit notes – a variation on more familiar schemes such as those in Poland and the Czech Republic. According to initial plans, credit notes representing a nominal value of Ft1–2 million each are to be issued, and citizens can acquire a share of 1–2 per cent in them. There will be no capital redemption, only payments of interest at the rate of 8 per cent to 10 per cent and for a period of 10 years. Under this scheme every adult citizen is to be granted an interest-free loan amounting to Ft100,000.

ECONOMIC PROSPECTS FOR 1993–94

After three years of declining economic performance, possible ways of restarting economic growth are being examined. The government seems to be over-optimistic. After stagnation or a maximum drop of 3 per cent in 1993, the government expects real GDP growth in 1994 to range between 2 per cent and 4 per cent. There are in fact some positive signs. In industry, for example, small firms (with up to 50 employees) doubled their production in 1992, increasing their share in overall industrial output from 6.5 per cent to 14 per cent. Another encouraging sign is the fact that the contraction of industrial output stopped after December 1991 if examined on a month-to-month basis. Recent figures indicate that unemployment seems to have peaked in early-1993. Additionally, the most recent change in exchange rate policy together with public sector measures to stimulate business and restructure ailing enterprises may have some expansionary impact. On the other hand, the recently unsatisfactory export performance frustrates the hopes for export-led growth, and still shrinking investment expenditures seem to reveal an overall pessimistic 'wait-and-see' attitude of the business sector. The latter may be attributed to the uncertainties arising from the frequent changes in the legal and institutional framework over the past three years, which have certainly been necessary but nevertheless rather incalculable.

In contrast to domestic business, foreign investors are optimistic, which is reflected by the sustained inflow of foreign capital (US$400 million in the first quarter of 1993). This is undoubtedly an indication of Hungary's favourable economic potential. However, in order to mobilise this potential, existing uncertainties have to be overcome. This will be necessary for starting sustainable economic growth.

2

Political Transformation

GJW Government Relations

Hungary, traditionally known for its experiments with relatively more individual and entrepreneurial freedom, has also been in the forefront of mastering the smooth transition to democracy. The rapid demise of the regime of the ageing communist leader János Kádár surprised even the most optimistic observers. While founders of FIDESZ, the first non-communist youth movement, were still being harassed by police in March of 1988, by the end of that year the formation of democratic political parties was an accomplished fact.

TRANSITION AND ELECTIONS

In 1989 the foundations of the current democratic system were laid down amidst a rapidly changing international environment. The parliament enacted (just as it had enacted anything brought before it by communist authorities) the basic laws of the transition. These laws, like the amendment of the Constitution, the law on the freedom of association and the freedom of assembly, the law on general elections and the law on political parties were brokered during months of hard negotiations between the democratic parties and communist representatives. A referendum in November 1989 opted for a president elected by parliament and excluded the possibility of a Communist president, setting the stage for total and unconditional transition.

The first free general elections in March 1990 and the election of the municipal assemblies therafter fulfilled the dream of many Hungarians – for the first time in history a free, independent and democratic Hungarian Republic was born. The total withdrawal of the Soviet troops from Hungary later in 1990 restored the national sovereignty that was terminated first by invading Nazi troops in 1944, then by Soviet 'liberators' during World War II and thereafter.

Following the 1990 elections a conservative three-party coalition, led by Prime Minister József Antall, the President of the Hungarian Democratic Forum, took charge of government. The Christian Democratic People's Party and the Smallholders' Party joined the government as junior partners.

The parliament elected Arpád Göncz, a well respected writer from the Alliance of Free Democrats – the major opposition party in the House – as President of Hungary. The two other opposition parties – the Alliance of Young Democrats (FIDESZ) and the party of the reformed communists (the Socialist Party) – completed the list of six parties elected to parliament in 1990. In the summer of 1993 a nationalist group broke away from the Hungarian Democratic Forum, increasing the number of parliamentary groups by one. Thus there are now seven factions in parliament plus an ever increasing group of independent MPs. The government's majority has dropped to a dangerous low but the votes of some independent MPs are likely to keep it in office until the end of its term in 1994. At the next elections, in May 1994, roughly half of the members of the single chamber parliament will be elected again in majoritarian single member constituencies, with the other half elected on proportional party lists.

POLITICAL INFRASTRUCTURE

The political system conceived by the negotiations of 1989 is a traditional continental parliamentary democracy, with a President as ceremonial head of state elected for a five-year term. Parliament elects the Prime Minister by a simple majority. The President appoints ministers upon the recommendation of the Prime Minister. A vote of confidence (if tabled by the opposition) can only be carried if a new Prime Minister is elected at the same time. A new government has to be formed if the government loses a vote of confidence of its own initiative.

A major new safeguard of the political stability of the country is the Constitutional Court which has already annulled several laws and regulations on constitutional grounds. Members of the Constitutional Court are elected for a 12-year period by a two-thirds majority of the parliament. Rulings of the Constitutional Court have introduced the only common law element to the otherwise continental Hungarian legal system. Meanwhile, the separation of powers has almost been completed and the government hopes to conclude legislation in this respect by the end of its term.

Printed media are controlled by a number of domestic and international publishers; the electronic media on the other hand are dominated by the government-controlled national channels. By Spring 1994 the first local channels will be licensed but national commercial channels are not expected to be launched until authorised by the next Parliament. As the government and opposition have failed to reach a consensus on this, it will be the task of the next government to pursue it further.

In its first three years the parliament has passed a variety of laws that establish the legal background for the economic and social transition. Concessions, accounting, gambling, bankruptcy, telecommunications, post, railways, electricity, banking and labour relations are among the many areas covered by legislation during the period. Parliament also passed several laws on the restitution of property nationalised by communist authorities. As opposed to developments in several other countries in the region, only a portion of agricultural land and the property of the churches were restituted in kind. All other claims were satisfied with compensation coupons that can be used to purchase goods, shares of companies or land. As a consequence, there is no uncertainty about ownership of industrial or residential real estate in Hungary.

The legal and political changes have affected not only the economy but all other spheres of life as well. New democratically elected local governments took control of local matters from the formerly powerful county administrations. The districts of the capital also gained significant independence from the City itself.

As a result of the events of the past five years, Hungary is a proper parliamentary democracy with democratic control over the government and its armed forces. Despite the heavy social and economic burden of the transition there is no political force that could or would threaten the country's political stability.

3
Hungary and its Potential
ETD Ltd

ORIGINS AND DEVELOPMENT

The Hungarians are part of a tiny linguistic group related to the Finns and Estonians. The warlike nomad Hungarians occupied the Carpathian Basin in the late-9th century and adopted Christianity by the end of the 10th century. When the Hungarians occupied the Carpathian Basin, they also extended their rule over a significantly larger population of Slavs, Germans and the remnants of the Avars. However, in defiance of received wisdom, the language of the ruling minority prevailed. Genetically, the Hungarians of today exhibit little more than 20 per cent of the ancient Magyar blood, yet the language is clearly the descendant of the old Finn-Ugrian Magyar.

Between 1000 and 1500 Hungary was the determining military power in central Europe, with a population greater than that of the British Isles. Its military strength was underpinned by a strong economy. For example, Hungary was the largest producer of gold in the known world at that time and remained so until the discovery of the Americas.

However, Hungary had to pay dearly for its strategic geographical location at the crossroads between east and west, north and south. For over 150 years from the 16th century onwards, Hungary was Europe's shield against the military might of the Ottoman Turks. When the Turkish wars ended in the second half of the 17th century, vast tracts of the country's fertile plains were totally depopulated by war and it was in the interests of the Hungarian landowners to import settlers from anywhere. A large migration of people into Hungary began, primarily from Wallachia (now Romania), Serbia, Bosnia, Germany and Bohemia. This large settlement of non-Hungarians was to lead eventually to the country's break-up under the Treaty of Versailles in 1919.

Hungary lost almost three-quarters of its territory and two-thirds of its population to three new countries: Czechoslovakia, Yugoslavia and Romania, as well as to Austria and the Ukraine. While this loss was an absolute catastrophe for Hungary, looking at it with the eyes of a potential British investor today, it can be argued that it renders Hungary a desirable target for investment as a hub for companies wishing to establish themselves in this region.

While the shortcomings of the Versailles Treaty are manifested in the murderous conflicts in former Yugoslavia or the more peaceful divorce between Czechs and Slovaks, in ethnically homogeneous Hungary there are no nationalistic tensions. In fact, Hungary is quite pragmatic about its territorial losses and successive governments have reiterated at every available opportunity that they have no territorial claims. Thanks to the wisdom of Miklós Németh's government of the late-1980s, Hungary's political transformation to full democracy was orderly and peaceful – by far the smoothest among the ex-communist countries.

Now there is parliamentary democracy, evidenced most clearly perhaps by the fact that the approaching elections in May 1994 have inspired public mud-slinging which is creating headlines and an excitable mood amongst politicians. There is infighting within the ruling coalition and a tendency for the largest party, the Democratic Forum, to hog television. It is most unlikely that the next election will produce a working majority for any single party and once again, therefore, there will be a coalition government in power.

THE HUNGARIAN DIASPORA

The number of Hungarians living in Hungary is almost exactly matched by the number living abroad. In this respect, some of the official statistics are misleading. For example, statistics variously show between 650,000 and 800,000 Hungarians in Slovakia. The real figure is around 1.6 million. After the war, when Hungarians were being deported from Slovakia along with Germans, a large number registered as Slovaks. Nevertheless, they still speak Hungarian at home, especially in areas where they are in a minority.

International companies have made use of this diaspora. For example, if a company opens a new factory in Hungary, it can easily lock into the markets in neighbouring countries via local, Hungarian dominated companies. This interlocking is beneficial for all and is probably the best tool for creating genuine understanding among the nations of the Carpathian Basin.

Hungarians have a reputation for hard work and strong, driving ambition. Compared to their numbers, it is amazing to see how many Hungarians are in the top echelons of so many fields, including music and high finance, such as Sir Georg Solti and George Soros. The team which developed the first atomic bomb in the US was dominated by Hungarians, and Hungary, size-for-size, is the most successful country in Olympic sports.

A good example of Hungarian work ethics can be seen in the former Yugoslav province of Vojvodina, which has a large Hungarian ethnic minority. There, even in Hungarian towns, the top politicians and most company chairmen are the ruling Serbs. However, key posts where hard work and technological innovation are needed are disproportionately filled by Hungarians. Nobody claims that the Hungarians are a super-race, but they seem prepared to do any amount of work in order to fulfil their ambitions. Indeed, they often try to solve problems by hard work alone, when politics might be more effective. Consequently Hungarians are generally bad politicians and are usually the last to retreat from fighting lost causes.

INDUSTRY, AGRICULTURE AND PRIVATISATION

The Hungarian pharmaceutical industry is a world power and Hungary is among the top four exporting countries in this field. Alkaloida is responsible for more than 10 per cent of the world production of morphine and Gedeon Richter accounts for over 20 per cent of pharmaceutical sales in the countries of the former Soviet Union.

Electronics and engineering are another strong area. Tungsram is one of the world's largest manufacturers of light bulbs and has been acquired by General Electric. The South Korean

Samsung has made significant strides in modernising the Orion television company in Jászfényszaru. Unilever and Henkel are making substantial investments in existing detergent plants, while one of the world's leading bus companies, Ikarus, has received investment from Russia. Even a company practising embalming is attracting interest from the UK.

Hungarian industry is currently one of the best investment targets for expanding companies. It has great traditions, skills, and in many cases an excellent raw material base. Yet because of the recent political and economic upheavals, superb Hungarian companies can be acquired for a fraction of the price of similar ones only a few hundred miles further west.

There are certain economic laws and patterns of human behaviour that seem to go hand-in-hand. Because Hungary has achieved greater liberalisation than its fellow members in Comecon, at the time when the wind of political change blew away the communist built superstructure, it had preserved its lead in economic transformation. Experience of the past few years has shown that by and large the Hungarian pattern is being followed by all former Comecon countries that have reasonably stable governments. It will take a few years for privatisation and the transformation of industry in Russia, the Ukraine, Romania and the other countries to reach the position where Hungary is now, by which time Hungary will be well on its way to integrating into the economy of Western Europe.

Agriculture and the food industry have been the main power-house of the Hungarian economy. While the former political system created great distortions in some industries, such as steel, mining and electronics, an exceptionally well-prepared group of technocrats took charge of the section of the economy managed by the Ministry of Agriculture and Food. Luckily these technocrats were strong politically and they were able to exert sufficient influence to receive both funding and backing from other ministries to realise their visions. The experts of the EC meat inspectorate in Brussels were surprised to find recently that the Hungarian meat industry was one of the most modern in the world, on a par with Denmark and in many respects well ahead of its German and British counterparts.

During part of the 1980s, and at the initiative of an Anglo-Hungarian, Béla Hidvégi, Hungary became the largest producer in Europe of both canned and frozen sweetcorn. Hidvégi established not only the new technology, but almost overnight created strong markets for Hungarian sweetcorn. In fact, as a result of the great floods in the US in 1993, Hungary exports significant quantities of this product to America.

North-east Hungary became the most intensive apple growing region in the world and around it several large and modern plants became serious market contenders in apple juice concentrate, canned apple products and even fruit-based baby foods. The technology and machinery were the best money could buy.

Progress of reform

The new government of József Antall began with a pragmatic approach to managing the Hungarian economy. They were not technocrats and were willing to listen to experts. Even privatisation started in a sober and well organised manner. The aim was orderly privatisation of as many companies as possible without undue strain on the viability of these companies. However, unexpected factors changed the situation. The combination of untreated economic ills and human behaviour rapidly changed the scene. The following three main factors started to cripple the whole economy:

- In the former planned economy companies were left with little working capital. This was a relatively small problem when borrowing carried an almost symbolic rate of interest. However, rapid inflation set in, fuelled by the introduction of personal income tax and value added tax. Both these taxes had strong inflationary effects, although here again Hungary did not end with the rates experienced in Poland, Romania or the former Soviet Union. Some industries are highly capital intensive. Interest rates rose to over 40 per cent. For many companies it was impossible to finance such high interest rates and, one-by-one, whole sections of industry were paralysed financially.

- The most noticeable feature of a planned economy is an almost complete lack of marketing expertise. There was not only an absence of imaginative packaging and advertising, but hardly any company had even a rudimentary marketing team. Technically competent management remained production oriented and highly intellectual experts failed to develop an awareness of even the most basic marketing skills. Some people believe that sales and marketing is a science. It is not. Good marketing is done by people with good common sense. Therefore it is baffling to see how slowly common sense sales skills are taking root among the leaders of Hungarian industry. The lack of expenditure on marketing is well illustrated by Table 3.1.

Table 3.1   *Business travel expenditure in 1992*

	Total expenditure ($ bn)	Expenditure per employee ($)
Belgium	4.0	1731
France	25.3	1443
Germany	38.8	1767
Hungary	**0.3**	**159**
Italy	16.0	1128
Netherlands	6.2	1773
Spain	8.8	1421
Sweden	6.8	2637
Switzerland	5.9	2331
UK	30.3	1422

■ The third factor will be the most lasting. While there are fast cures for financial instability and marketing problems, it is almost impossible to remedy the destructive effects of ignorant political interference.

Land ownership was always an emotional issue, but compared to other countries, privatisation in Hungary started in a realistic atmosphere. Unfortunately the former leader of the second largest party in the coalition government, Torgyán, started an unstoppable avalanche. Everybody wanted land. The resultant pressures on co-operatives and state farms came in addition to their liquidity problems causing a rapid, albeit temporary decline of Hungarian agricultural efficiency.

The destabilising influence of land privatisation affected two million people: a huge number in a country with a population of approximately 10 million. It is expected that 75 per cent of agricultural land will end up in private hands, but 75 to 80 per cent of this will be in the ownership of people who are not involved in its cultivation.

In the meantime, privatisation of industry has suffered bureaucratic delays. When there was need for quick decisions, the issues were lost among the State Property Agency (SPA), the Ministry of Agriculture, the Ministry of Industry and the Ministry of Finance. Criticism of the system caused officialdom and particularly the SPA to escape behind impenetrable barricades of bureaucracy. As a result, when quick decisions could save a company, delayed reactions that could take a year or more pushed many superb firms to the edge of destruction. It is difficult to demand results from destabilised management fearful of inexperienced distant bureaucrats. Delays often meant that the sale price fell to a fraction of what could have been attained by decisive handling of the privatisation.

The residual power of communist-style foreign trade companies was also destructive. In 1992 the grain and food merchants Agrimpex, Gabona RT or Terimpex each produced profits of US$7 to US$8 million, while 1200 agricultural cooperatives together showed profits of around US$14 million and 126 state farms lost US$11 million.

Those branches of industry that rely strongly on an agricultural base have suffered the most. Secondary processors are expected to thrive. For example, in 1990 the meat industry produced US$5 million more than the brewing industry, but by 1991 the brewing industry was leading by US$45 million.

The most recent danger, again fuelled by the pre-election rhetoric of political ignorance, is economic nationalism. Even official SPA publications are saying that 'foreign capital retards domestic production'. The most ridiculous assertion is that multinationals move to Hungary in order to liquidate their competitors there. Yet the same publication admits that the problem is not loss of markets but lack of capital and that 25 to 30 per cent foreign ownership of a section of industry is good.

In the first 8 months of 1993 the value of Hungarian exports fell dramatically: their value to the end of August 1993 was US$5.248 billion, signalling a 25 per cent drop in comparison to the same period last year. In the same period the year before, imports to the value of US$7.569 billion arrived in the country (this is a 2.1 per cent increase over the first 8 months of 1992), which means that the foreign trade deficit reached US$2.321 billion by the end of August. The drop in agricultural and food exports was particularly serious: according to data from the Ministry of International Economic Relations, exports in this area plummeted by 37.4 per cent.

Successes of the transition

Of course, not all is doom and gloom. For example, the world's most efficient integrated poultry company, Bernard Matthews Plc, was recently established in Hungary. This was made easier by the active support of the government, which realised the immense benefit that can flow from the presence of such a company. It is of special value that this major investment happened in one of the worst crisis areas in the food industry. Bernard Matthews has acquired the poultry company in Sárvár, which will go through spectacular development during the next few years.

It is unfortunate that the vegetable oil industry was acquired in its entirety by Feruzzi in partnership with Unilever. Feruzzi is a financially unstable Italian conglomerate. (The privatisation was well-handled by SPA). However, Unilever's presence is decidedly positive and extends to other industries besides the production of margarine and detergents. Nestlé is the other multinational which showed an early presence: its main acquisition was the Szerencs chocolate company. It is surprising that they have not opposed Unilever more aggressively in the ice cream industry.

In the canning industry Heinz and Hillsdown jointly bought the canning company at Kecskemét. Since this is the most important Hungarian producer of baby foods, they have stolen a march on Nestlé. These companies and several other astute firms realised that the transitional upheavals are only temporary. In fact the problems described render their investments even more cost effective and their new acquisitions hugely profitable.

Apart from strong traditions, Hungarian industry has so many outstanding qualities that it will emerge from the difficulties of its current transformation with renewed strength. The climate, the underlying strong base and the country's central position in relation to its most profitable markets are there. The professional standard and level of education of management on average is high. Hungarians have positive work ethics. All this combined with the grossly undervalued facilities of good companies, make Hungarian industry one of the most desirable takeover targets.

A refreshing breath of fresh air in the economic climate is emerging from the recently formed State Asset Management

Company (AV Rt), which is not yet bureaucratic. Its recently appointed Managing Director, Szabolcs Szekeres, was excellent, but after a few months he was eased out. In a surprise move, Lajos Csepi, hitherto Managing Director of the SPA, took over AV Rt in January 1994. Since he manages close to 60 per cent of Hungarian industry and all the state owned banks, his influence is going to be crucial in the years to come.

The Hungarian economy is thought to have bottomed out in 1993 and currently to be the best and safest investment in Central and Eastern Europe. The rhetoric of economic nationalism will die after the forthcoming elections and foreign companies will once again be the white knights of Hungarian industry.

4

A New Legal Framework

SJ Berwin & Co

The aim of this chapter is to describe the legislative process, to explain the composition of parliament and government and to provide an overview of the political and traditional legislative framework in which the transition towards a market economy is taking place.

THE LEGAL INFRASTRUCTURE

The Constitution

Hungary has a written Constitution which was the first legislative creation of the new parliament in the summer of 1990. The Constitution's pre-eminent position in the legislative framework is protected by the requirement that any amendments to it must have a two-thirds majority in parliament. The role of the Constitution is of central importance to the law of Hungary because all other laws are to be construed as complying with, and being in accordance with, the Constitution. Consequently, any right provided by the Constitution which is breached either by the action of another person or a legislative provision is actionable as such; and any law which ignores or is contrary to a basic tenet of the Constitution, or which purports to deny or remove rights granted by the Constitution, is void and of no effect.

There are two declarations which are central to the Hungarian Constitution. They provide that the state is founded upon a market economy and, as a result, public and private property are to receive equal protection before the law. Further, the right to take part in economic enterprise is acknowledged, together with the need for freedom of competition. On a more personal or individual level, the principal tenet of the Constitution is that the state is a republic in which the ultimate sovereignty rests with the people. They exercise this sovereignty via their elected representatives.

The right to form political parties is also given prominence, and political parties can be formed without sanction or control, although there are positions to which an officer or member of a political party may not be appointed (for example, as a judge in the Constitutional Court). Trade unions are expressly vested with the duty of protecting and representing the interests of employees, co-operatives and entrepreneurs.

The Constitution also lays down basic human rights that are protected by the courts. It provides for protection from discrimination on grounds of sex, race, religion and other similar grounds. This is important given the ethnic diversity of the Hungarian people. All Hungarians are granted the freedom to choose their employment and to receive equal pay for equal work. They also have the right to strike and to form organisations for the protection of human and social rights. Importantly, private property rights are guaranteed, with official expropriation permitted only where it is in the public interest.

Parliament

Parliament is the supreme organ of power in Hungary and comprises the people's elected representatives. The competence of parliament covers the following areas:

- the initiation of legislation;

- the definition of the state's social and economic goals;

- the approval of the budget and the balancing of state finances;

- the examination and enactment of the government's proposed legislation;

- the ratification of international treaties entered into on the state's behalf;

- the declaration of war and/or the proclamation of a state of emergency in cases of the threat of armed attack by foreign powers or the threat of anti-constitutional violence from within the state; and

- the election of the President, the Prime Minister, the President of the Supreme Court and the members of the Constitutional Court.

Parliament is elected for a term of four years. No members of parliament are allowed to become President or members of the Constitutional Court. The parliamentary speaker is elected from among the members.

Parliament creates standing committees from among its members and can instruct them to investigate any question the members generally think necessary. Any data requested by a standing committee must be supplied and anyone called to give evidence before a standing committee is obliged to do so.

Parliament passes legislation with the assent of more than half the votes of the members present. Parliament only has a quorum to conduct its business when more than half of the members are present. There are specific instances where two-thirds of the members are required to approve specific legislation – for example, to alter the Constitution. Any member of parliament can initiate legislation. This holds true for the President, any member of the government or even a parliamentary committee. The members can dissolve parliament by a two-thirds majority vote, and the President can dissolve it where the parliament has denied a vote of confidence in the government 4 times within the preceding 12 months.

Delegated legislation

The government has it within its power to issue decrees and pass resolutions which then have an effect equivalent to that of delegated legislation. The only limitation on the power of the government in this respect is that it cannot contravene any of the laws passed by parliament, nor the Constitution.

GOVERNMENT STRUCTURE

The President

The President is the head of state. He is elected by parliament for a term of five years. To stand, the individual must be a citizen who is entitled to vote and aged not less than 35 on election day. Any one individual can only hold the position for two terms.

Legislation only becomes effective when it is endorsed by the

President. When a measure is passed by parliament, the President has 15 (or 5 days if the speaker so requests) to refuse to endorse the legislation. At this point he can refer it back to the parliament for reconsideration. If the measure is passed again by parliament, the President is required to endorse it within 5 days. The only circumstance in which the President can refuse to endorse the measure at this stage is if he considers it to be unconstitutional, in which case he can send it to the Constitutional Court for consideration.

The duties of the President include the following:

- to conclude international treaties on behalf of the state;

- to set the dates for parlimentary elections and also for local government elections;

- to participate in full parliamentary meetings and parliamentary committee meetings;

- to propose the taking of measures by parliament; and

- to motion for a plebiscite.

The President can be removed from office by a vote of two-thirds of the members, by his own resignation, or where he transgresses a law or the Constitution (as decided by the Constitutional Court).

If for any reason the President becomes incapacitated, the speaker assumes his duties, although without the powers to delay legislation or dissolve parliament.

The Prime Minister

The government comprises the Prime Minister and his ministers. The Prime Minister is elected by a simple majority of the members of parliament. At the same time, parliament decides on the acceptance of a government programme of legislation. It is a feature of the legal framework aimed at facilitating the shift to a market economy that the emphasis is still very much on the adoption and pursuit of economic programmes.

The Prime Minister can be removed, and indeed replaced, by a vote of 'no confidence' supported by the votes of the majority of the members. A candidate named in his place by the same motion takes office immediately and installs a new government.

Government ministers are proposed by the Prime Minister

and their appointment is effected by the President. The duties of the newly constituted government include the protection of citizens' rights, the implementation of laws, the creation of economic plans, the determination of foreign policy and the overseeing of the operation of all departments in accordance with the policy determined by and with authority delegated from the government.

NON-GOVERNMENTAL ORGANISATIONS

The State Audit Office

The State Audit Office performs the financial and economic accounting functions of the parliament. Its duties are two-fold. First, to oversee the management of state finances, and secondly to scrutinise the efficacy of the proposed budget. It also oversees the management of state assets. The office reports its findings in an annual report, which the President submits to parliament. All of its findings are then made public. The State Audit Office president is elected by two-thirds of the members of parliament.

The central bank

The National Bank of Hungary is the central bank of issue in the Hungarian Republic. Its constitutional role hinges on the following duties:

- to issue legal tender;
- to protect the stability of the national currency; and
- to regulate the circulation of money.

The president of the National Bank is appointed for a six-year term by the President of the Republic. The Bank's president must make an annual report to parliament.

The Bank also oversees the establishment and control of commercial banks and insurance companies.

THE LEGAL SYSTEM

The courts

The Constitutional Court has as its primary obligation to uphold, enforce and interpret the Constitution. It has the power to annul any law passed by parliament if it considers it to violate any role or principle of the Constitution. Anyone can bring such an action before the Constitutional Court provided they can show their claim falls within the Court's jurisdiction. The 15 judges of the Constitutional Court are nominated by a committee composed of one representative of each political party with seats in parliament.

The judges of the Supreme Court, county courts and local courts comprise professional judges and lay assessors. The Supreme Court creates guidelines for the conduct of proceedings and the administration of justice in the other courts. Further, all of its decisions and directives are binding on the lower courts. The president of the Supreme Court is nominated by the President of the Hungarian Republic and must then be elected by two-thirds of the parliament. It then falls to the Supreme Court president to appoint professional judges for the courts. Judges are independent and must not have any affiliations to a political party, nor can they carry on any political activities.

Arbitration

Arbitration (the system for resolving disputes arising out of international commercial transactions) is now well-established in Hungary. The Hungarian Court of Arbitration is attached to the Hungarian Chamber of Commerce and Industry and has been in existence for almost 40 years. Although the greatest proportion of its cases arise out of intra-Comecon trade, the Court has accepted cases involving foreigners and recently has had referrals of an increasing number of cases involving Western partners.

The rules of the Court are modelled on the arbitration of the United Nations Commission for International Trade Law (Uncitral) and the government has indicated its intention to adopt a new Hungarian arbitration law based on the Uncitral Model Law on International Commercial Arbitration. Hungary is party to the major international conventions concerning arbitrations, which facilitate the implementation of arbitrators' decisions.

At the present time, disputes can only go to arbitration where:

- the dispute is between a Hungarian economic organisation and a foreign party; or
- the dispute is between two foreign parties; and
- the parties have expressly agreed in writing to submit the dispute to arbitration.

Where the parties have agreed to go to arbitration, they are prevented from seeking any other form of redress, unless the use or result of the arbitral proceedings can be shown to have been in some way unlawful.

The Hungarian Court of Arbitration can enforce any judgment involving foreign partners that is within the jurisdiction of the ordinary commercial courts.

The civil law tradition

Hungarian law is based upon the continental civil law system and is therefore codified.

The Hungarian Civil Code covers the principal rules of civil relations (property law, contract law, etc) and is the basis of all civil law. However, there are many statutes and ministerial regulations which apply or explain the specific rules of the Civil Code, (for example, the specific rules relating to a foreign trade contract). As a result, the law for specific subjects must be gathered from various sources. The system of civil law can be seen to be vertical, with lower legislation being subordinated to the higher – ie a statute being subordinated to the Civil Code with the Constitution thereafter always taking precedence. A particular difficulty at present, however, is that legislation is continually being modified to conform to the new political and economic system.

The structure of the Civil Code is important. It contains two types of provisions – mandatory and dispositive (distinguished by use of the words 'shall' or 'may'). Every term of a contract which is contrary to the mandatory rules will be either null and void or unenforceable depending upon the provisions of the code itself. Dispositive rules will provide the terms for a contract if the parties do not agree otherwise. This means in commercial transactions that every undesirable or impractical dispositive rule must be clearly and expressly excluded or substituted by an appropriate contractual term, otherwise it will apply.

Treaty arrangements

Hungarian law declares itself to be subject to the recognised rules of international law. The legal system undertakes to harmonise itself with the obligations imposed on Hungary by its participation in international treaties.

5

Hungarian Business Culture

KPMG Peat Marwick

Hungary was the first country in the region to introduce reforms which, as long ago as 1968, introduced managerial autonomy for companies. It boasts a strong tradition of private enterprise. Caught in a macroeconomic tidal wave, its people have shown themselves to be adaptable and resourceful. According to the Hungarian tax office, companies employing less than 100 people have generated about 40 per cent of GDP, while 20 per cent is accounted for by companies with foreign participation. The legacy of openness and enterprise has pulled in large inflows of capital in recent years. Hungarian industry has had some success in compensating for the collapse of its Eastern export markets and shifting exports to the West.

It is hoped that the Budapest Stock Exchange will eventually play its role as allocator of capital efficiently. At the moment the government is reluctant to float companies on the Stock Exchange because of economic problems and its determination to attract direct foreign investment. After the frenzy of the initial phases of privatisation, Hungary seems to be coming down to earth as a country of approximately 11 million people with a small and hopefully prosperous economy in the future.

PRIVATE ENTERPRISE

Indigenous talent

Overall industrial production in 1993 is still below what it was in 1988, and official GDP is 17 per cent below the level of 5 years ago. However, statistics have failed to register the growth of small private businesses. The dynamism of the private sector relies on more than anecdotal evidence such as family-owned shops lining the streets of Budapest and the lively trade in private imports of cars from Germany. There are more than 600,000 one-person businesses, mainly tradesmen and shop-keepers. Private enterprise is predominant in the artisan, handicraft and service industries. In the past, entrepreneurial talent could only be applied in the black economy. This tradition of a parallel economy is often cited as a firm foundation for the growth of a market economy, because its participants knew and understood very well the concept of consumer demand and profits, albeit on a cash basis. The picture is still relatively unclear – there is a reluctance to register or pay taxes. Private businesses tend to be small and still in their infancy. Their growth will be hampered by the unwillingness of banks to lend or, when they do, by excessive interest rates.

At the other end of the spectrum there are a few big private companies such as Kontrax and Müszertechnika (both involved in office equipment and telecommunications) and Fotex, which started off in photographic processing facilities and now has expanded its interests to retailing, contact lenses and crystal ware production. Müszertechnika is one of the oldest private companies – it started making its own computers and later shifted into the production of IBM compatibles. One of its subsidiaries, MT Display, has sold equipment to Taiwan. These companies are growing very fast and analysts wonder if rapid diversification is not overstretching management. Kontrax, now in bankruptcy, was converted in 1992 into a holding company and two of its subsidiaries were listed on the Budapest Stock Exchange. The company was growing too fast and this led to its inability to service its debts and a serious liquidity crisis. The company identified its problems as poor monitoring of costs and inadequate cash flow planning.

Government is seeking alternative ways to expand domestic shareholding and create more interest in the companies left on its books. Flotations on the stock exchange have been hampered by the economic climate. Management buy-outs, instalment sales and lease privatisations lessen the need for upfront cash. Lease privatisations, if they go well, can enable an individual or a group of individuals to control a state-owned company and to operate for a set period, after which they will become the owners. However, Hungarians have not yet taken up the running.

Institutional and small investors have steered clear of equity. Progress is being hampered by lack of business confidence.

Foreign capital

There has been a hint of a gold rush about the flow of foreign investment to Hungary. Although people expecting to get rich quick may be disappointed, companies which have made investments long term can expect profits. Foreign investors are generally looking to acquire significant market share of manufacturing and processing capacity. Hungarian companies need modern technology, know-how and managerial assistance. However, foreign multinationals have their earnings under pressure and at the moment are not in an acquisitive mood. The sham joint ventures, set up to enable Hungarians to import cars duty-free or take advantage of tax holidays, used to be a very common occurrence, but are on the way out now as the government has created a more level playing field.

Styl is a successful company. It is the largest employer in the textiles sector and 95 per cent of its production is exported (and most of this for high quality labels). The workers received 10 per cent of the shares when the company was privatised but most of them sold their stock and foreigners now own 98 per cent of the company.

THE STATE SECTOR

The falling share of the state sector in GDP is expected and is desirable in the long run. It indicates that the economy is being restructured. Particularly problematic is the situation of larger enterprises with no foreign buyer in sight. Enterprises have been required to transform themselves into a corporate form as a prelude to privatisation. Profits should now be their prime motivation, but even if they are potentially viable, they remain heavily geared and lacking in confidence. Many are good at manufacturing but not at sales and marketing. An appreciation of the legacy of central planning and the effects of inertia in resisting change is crucial to understanding changes required in attitudes.

A few state-owned companies have taken the bull by the horns and actively sought or are seeking their own foreign partner. A new class of institutional shareholder, such as the Social

Security Directorate which was handed billions of forints worth of assets to fund social security needs, are unlikely to make a company successful, because they are unlikely to force companies to perform.

Management culture

Since the adoption of the Law on Councils in 1984, which introduced self management to most enterprises, managers have asserted their prerogatives over the enterprises they managed. Whereas in Poland workers councils asserted themselves where the state had deserted control, managers in Hungary play a crucial role in the governance of enterprises and in the corporatisation and privatisation process. They can initiate and prepare the transformation of their enterprises, although the SPA can veto their plans. In practice the SPA leaves much of the actual work, including finding buyers, to managers and gets involved in negotiating the more controversial cases.

THE PROFESSIONS

Accountants

A large number of people are called accountants, but their training and experience has been mainly in recording information, not in its analysis. The market is concentrated – currently the six major international accounting firms account for most professional services to large or international companies. Hungarian firms do exist, but are unlikely to provide services to international clients. They provide bookkeeping and other services to smaller clients. However, as the economy settles down, it is possible that small firms will merge in order to compete.

The Association of Hungarian Auditors was set up in 1987. It has over 1000 members and is likely to evolve as the primary professional body for accountants. Of primary concern is training of new accountants and also teaching businesses just what the firms have to offer. Priority is being given to developments in the theory and practice of financial reporting, but practising accountants will make little impact if staff within the companies themselves do not understand the nature and purpose of financial information and fail to appreciate the importance of management information.

Lawyers

The domestic profession is going through a traumatic process of restructuring as the two main branches, attorneys and the legal advisers, are in the process of forming a united profession. Foreigners are barred from practising Hungarian law. Many local lawyers have already benefited from links with foreign firms establishing a presence in Budapest and through work being referred to them. But they lack the international experience required when dealing with trans-border transactions. There have been accusations that they are only used to sign papers and thus comply with regulations, but there are a number of strong local firms emerging.

6

Market Intelligence

KPMG Peat Marwick

Hungary has been familiar for a longer period of time with the workings of a market economy than its Comecon neighbours. However, economic activities were still carried on within the constraints of a command economy, and the information requirements of the state are not relevant to enterprises. Consequently, reliable and consistent business information was hard to obtain.

This can make life awkward for the foreign business person used to finding information from extensive sources at the touch of a button. However, in the last two years, business information on Hungary has become more available and of better quality. There is a wide range of material from domestic sources – directories and investment guides, business journals and statistics. This chapter is not intended to be a definitive guide as there is a constantly improving range of products and information services.

PUBLICATIONS

There are many periodicals devoted to Central and Eastern Europe and there is not enough space here to mention them all. An annual paperback directory, *East European Business Information*, provides a comprehensive overview of the major sources of information, but it is restricted to sources of information in the English language. Both FT Publications and the Economist Intelligent Unit have a good selection of publications ranging from newsletters to reports on specific sectors of industry such as insurance, energy and construction.

There are a number of publications devoted specifically to Hungary, such as economic and business journals and legal monitors. These give insights into the business environment and Hungary's economic environment and discuss changes in legislation and their likely impact. A number of these publications have a 'matchmaking' page that lists companies seeking partners or co-operation arrangements. These vary in their rate of publication and the depth of analysis provided. Here we can mention *Econews* (a daily from the Hungarian News Agency), *Business Partner Hungary*, the *Hungarian Market Report*, the *Hungarian Economic Review* (a glossy magazine published by the Hungarian Chamber of Commerce) and the *Hungarian Financial Review*.

STATISTICS AND CONSUMER MARKET INFORMATION

Much has changed since the days of central planning. Hungary now reports to the IMF and other international institutions and economic data and indicators are being brought into line with OECD standards, but comparisons with the past should be treated carefully. There are sharp discontinuities as changes in methodology, classification and data collection are implemented.

GDP figures throughout Central and Eastern Europe are notoriously controversial. Figures will depend very much on whether the source is domestic or derives from an international institution. Coverage of the private sector economy is still very poor. Hungary's statistics do not show the economic activities of firms with less than 50 employees. They show a large contraction in national income, which, although real, understates the contribution of small-scale private business in terms of output, sales, employment and investments. Many of these businesses conduct small-scale activities, usually in cash, and are reluctant to declare their real income. Informal trade goes unreported in order to evade customs duties. This makes foreign trade figures unreliable. Similarly, foreign currency receipts are not banked – so how can one measure local foreign exchange holdings? This makes the task of determining local purchasing power or set wages for local staff difficult. Available statistics should not be used to try and obtain an absolute picture of market size, but clear trends are emerging.

The Hungarian Central Statistical Office (CSO) is a vast bureaucratic organisation churning out statistics. It produces many publications, though only two in English. The major source of statistics is the *Hungarian Statistical Yearbook*, covering population, employment, income, investment, trade, production, etc. The *Statistical Pocketbook of Hungary* is a shorter version of the *Yearbook*. There is often an important time lag before statistics for a particular year are published, which may cause problems when the economy is undergoing rapid changes. With funds available from the EC PHARE programme, the CSO is upgrading its facilities. The aim is to provide reliable and up-to-date information for the Hungarian government, international institutions and private users. The National Bank of Hungary also publishes monthly and annual statistical bulletins in English.

A country report was published in 1993 by Eurostat in conjunction with the German Federal Statistical Office, which provides a useful statistical overview of Hungary. The OECD publishes a quarterly collection of short-term economic indicators, including trends in money supply, foreign trade and monthly wages. The Ministry of Trade publishes statistics on what is produced, exported and imported, and the destination of exports.

MARKET SURVEYS

To feel the pulse of popular moods and tastes and gauge market size or structure, surveys will need to be specifically commissioned. Evidence suggests that there is a high level of pent up demand for many consumer goods but the market is small, disposable incomes low and demand selective. There is no ready market although some Western brands, particularly in the fields of fashion, soft drinks and electronic goods, achieve a high level of recognition. Demand for such information has produced many small market research firms and polling organisations. Response rates to pollsters are still very high because expressing an opinion on jeans, yoghurts or politicians is still a novelty. The Hungarian Institute for Market Research and Kopint-Dataorg provide *ad hoc* market research. The Institute of Market Research maintains a sample of 60,000 people on its panel, while international market research companies are also offering services in Hungary. Gallup has a presence in Budapest through a joint venture called Mareco.

A more traditional means of researching the market is to take advantage of the trade fairs. These provide the opportunity to meet customers and observe the standard of competition.

COMPANY INFORMATION

There is an expanding range of company directories and databases. Most of these provide only basic company data such as name, address and telephone number. Sometimes they also give legal status, the number of employees and statistical codes for products according to the CSO classification. The *Hungarian Chamber of Commerce Business Directory* produces one such directory. In addition, two directories produced in the West, *Kompass* and *Dun and Bradstreet*, are available.

The Ministry of Trade maintains company databases giving contact details, legal status of the company and number of employees. The State Property Agency (SPA) issues lists of companies to be privatised, including the names of chief executives and other management team members, and details of accounts that must be submitted by applicants. It will also inform investors which companies are required to maintain partial state involvement. But it is generally difficult to find out more (eg, detailed company accounts). The Court of Registration registers all businesses with legal personality. This gives the names of shareholders in the case of a limited liability company and indications of changes in ownership. Unfortunately, this information cannot yet be matched with codes used by the CSO.

With regard to foreign direct investment and joint ventures (which at the moment are the main purchasers of capital goods), there is no comprehensive source regarding enterprises involved or the amount of capital invested. Since January 1992, data on the industry and country of origin of foreign investors have been collated by the CSO.

The growing importance of the stock market in the economy will mean that more financial data on companies will become available. Quoted companies have to publish accounts under Stock Exchange regulations, and Extel cards for some Hungarian companies can be found. Now in its third year, the *Hungarian Financial and Stock Exchange Almanac* provides information on banks, leasing and securities companies, auditing, consulting and corporate recovery firms. The almanac covers both Hungarian and foreign firms and this year it contains 800 entries.

There still remains a large body of companies for which financial data are not accessible. Credit reports and general financial data are not readily available for the majority of companies. Dun and Bradstreet has entered into a joint venture with the Hungarian company, HIT Investcenter Tradeinform, one of the subsidiaries of Kopint-Dataorg, which will probably mean greater availability of company balance sheet data and a more widespread distribution of business and credit management information.

TRADE AND PROFESSIONAL ORGANISATIONS

There are more than 30 active professional associations representing various sectors of the Hungarian economy. These involve companies (regardless of their ownership form) in such sectors as food processing, engineering, pharmaceuticals, building contractors, metallurgical industry and computer software. Change in the Hungarian economy is reflected in the growing share of privately owned companies in these associations. Other nation-wide organisations such as the National Association for Entrepreneurs, the Association of Hungarian Manufacturers and the Joint Venture Association also provide a number of contact points for new entrants to the market. Information on companies to be privatised and on the mechanics of privatisation can be obtained from SPA.

The Hungarian Chamber of Commerce has been in existence for over 100 years and, even during the years of economic centralisation and planning, it maintained contacts with other chambers of commerce and provided a link for its members with the world economy. Staff are helpful and courteous and most speak another European language. The Chamber provides *ad hoc* consultations and numerous publications. Regional chambers maintain contacts with local councils and lobby for better local facilities and on matters relating to local taxation. They also undertake other services such as the issue and certification of documents for international trade purposes and certificates of origin. Some offer business matching services for companies looking for trading partners or co-operation. They also participate to a large extent in the education of private entrepreneurs to help them deal with their new role as employers and taxpayers.

There are numerous accounting and consulting firms operating in Hungary (many of which have offices in London) that can give advice on registration, tax issues and finance. Those without experience of business in the region may find it useful to contact the Commercial Counsellor at the Hungarian Embassy.

7

Hungary and its Trading Partners

GJW Government Relations

GENERAL TRENDS

Hungary is a relatively open economy. The share of merchandise exports in GDP has oscillated between 33 per cent and 39 per cent in the late-1980s and early-1990s, reflecting a country with a small economy that must take an active role in international trade.

Hungarian foreign trade has suffered a major shock in recent years. With the 1990 collapse of the economic organisation of the Eastern European countries and the then Soviet Union (Comecon), trade flows have changed direction in a relatively short period of time. Whereas in 1989 41.6 per cent of Hungary's exports were still directed to Comecon countries (this figure itself about 10 percentage points lower than the peak of the mid-1980s), in 1992 the former Comecon area accounted for only 23.2 per cent of Hungarian exports. Similar trends were also observed in imports.

At present Hungary's major trading partner is the EC, accounting for over 50 per cent of exports and 45 per cent of imports. The redirection of trade between 1989 and 1992 was accompanied by a spectacular boom in export value. Calculated in dollars, exports grew by 15.5 per cent in 1990, by 37 per cent in 1991 and by 7.4 per cent in 1992. This was achieved in a continuously shrinking economy and while economic growth was generally decelerating in the most significant trading partners (Germany, Italy, Austria and Switzerland).

Exports

Rather than the result of an export stimulation policy, the rapid growth of exports is a consequence of spontaneous adaptation by exporting companies and of improvements in market access to most trading partners deriving from bilateral or multilateral agreements. Exporting firms can make use of a relatively modest range of export incentives, and exchange rate policy aimed at fighting inflation led to a slight revaluation in real terms throughout the 1989–92 period.

Over 70 per cent of exports are directed to industrialised markets. The share to developing countries is falling rapidly and reached a low of 5 per cent in 1992 as opposed to 9 per cent in 1991. It is worth noting that the value of exports to former Comecon countries increased by 14.3 per cent in 1992, indicating a possible overshooting in the trade redirecting process.

The structure of exports does not reflect a very advanced economy. In 1992 35 per cent of exports still consisted of raw materials and semi-finished goods. Agricultural produce accounted for 24 per cent and engineering products for 12 per cent. In 1992 the most dynamic export sectors were energy carriers (a 60 per cent increase on 1991 in dollar terms) and consumer goods (25 per cent growth).

Imports

Beginning from the late-1980s, Hungary has embarked consistently upon an import liberalisation policy. Over 90 per cent of imports have already been liberalised, and the tariffs have gradually been reduced. This resulted in quite dynamic growth in imports. Dollar imports almost doubled (they grew by 95 per cent) between 1989 and 1992. Non-convertible trade dropped to marginal levels in that period, imports falling from Ft158.2 billion in 1990 to a mere Ft1 billion in 1992.

The majority of imports – almost 70 per cent – came from industrialised countries, with the EC accounting for 42.7 per cent in 1992. Imports did not increase between 1991 and 1992, reflecting domestic recession. The increase of the share of imports in total domestic sales (import crowding-out) reached 8 per cent in 1991 and 4 per cent in 1992. Machinery and equipment are the biggest commodity group in imports with about 35 per cent of the total, followed by chemicals and light industry products (textiles, garments, footwear). The most dynamic import product groups are food industry products (although from a very low basis) and chemicals. Imports from the industrialised countries are dominated by machinery and consumer goods. Food products, minerals and chemicals imported from the EC showed considerable dynamism in 1992.

Trade balance

Hungary, being heavily indebted, made special efforts to produce trade balance surpluses in the 1980s. Various incentives and a very pronounced export increasing policy priority resulted in marginal dollar trade surpluses each year between 1987 and 1990. In 1991, as a result of Comecon trade being accounted for in dollars and fast growing imports, the trade balance showed a significant deficit at over US$1.1 billion. Considering the economic recession in that year and also in 1992, import surpluses evolved from consumer demand rather than from imports of investment inputs. The trade deficit was considerably less at US$356 million in 1992. In that year, trade with the EC and with the developing countries showed sizeable surpluses (US$604 million and US$101 million respectively) but deficits were registered in trade with EFTA (US$700 million) and with former Comecon countries (US$295 million).

Trade balance deficits were more than offset by direct capital investment and the contribution of tourism in 1991 and 1992. Data for 1993, however, indicate a sharp contrast to earlier export dynamism. In the first 5 months of 1993 exports were 27 per cent lower than in 1992. The trade balance deficit exceeded US$1 billion in mid-1993, with a shift to deficits with all major trading regions. For example, the first quarter 1993 figures showed that Hungary did not have a trade surplus with a single EC member country.

Trade policy will have to encompass more efficient methods of export promotion in order for Hungary to avoid the emergence of severe current account problems again.

HUNGARY'S TRADE WITH THE EC

Trade with the European Community, Hungary's most important trading partner, is crucial in assessing the trade performance of the Hungarian economy. The eminent role of the EC, besides trade share, is further underlined by two other factors. It

Table 7.1   *The direction of Hungarian trade (US$m), 1991–92*

	Exports		Imports		Trade balance	
	1991	*1992*	*1991*	*1992*	*1991*	*1992*
Industrial countries of which:	6,929	7,637	7,574	7,722	−644	−84.6
EC	4,661	5,331	4,673	4,732	−11	598.4
EFTA	1,528	1,575	2,180	2,282	−652	−706
Former Comecon of which:	2,181	2,494	2,449	2,789	−267	−295
CIS	1,200	1,407	1,590	1,863	−390	−456
Total	9,471	1,407	11,089	11,066	−1,117	−356

Source: Kopint-Datorg.

was one of the two most dynamic export markets for Hungary in 1992 (the other being former Comecon countries) with exports to the EC growing by 14.3 per cent; and it was also the region with by far the biggest Hungarian trade surplus in 1992.

Hungary concluded an Association Agreement with the EC in late-1991. Its foreign trade regulating chapters came into force as a Temporary Agreement in March 1992. These replaced the GSP clauses that were unilaterally extended to Hungary in 1990. The agreement with the Community does not offer many unilateral concessions to Hungary as an exporter. It is based on mutual opening of domestic markets, with asymmetry by way of the Hungarian side being committed to gradual abolition of trade barriers later than the EC. While according to some calculations the agreement resulted in a tariff reduction gain worth US$260 million for Hungary between March and December 1992 alone, other analysts spell out that Hungary might have fared better in the short run with the GSP clauses remaining in force.

The main points of the trade agreements concerning Hungarian exports to the EC are the following:

1. Non-agricultural exports (about 75 per cent of total Hungarian exports to the EC), will face no trade barriers after the transition period of 10 years.

2. Exports of general industrial products (about 55 per cent), will be exported under very favourable conditions. About 72–75 per cent of the group will be exported duty-free immediately. The rest, comprising vulnerable goods like

cars, buses, electric bulbs and toys, will become duty-free within 5 years. Quotas are set in this category and export volumes within them are practically duty-free immediately. Quotas will grow at 15 per cent pa for 5 years. Trade in these products will have about equal terms as in the GSP system.

3. Textiles and garment exports (about 15 per cent of total exports) will be subject to non-tariff barriers (quotas, quantitative restrictions) and tariffs. Tariffs will be eliminated in 7 years but contracted-out production from EC-origin raw materials will be immediately duty-free.

4. Tariffs on steel products (about 5 per cent of Hungarian exports) will be abolished in 5 years. Quantitative restrictions are immediately withdrawn.

5. Agricultural trade will not have general rules. The parties, while retaining their own agricultural trade policies, will agree on a case-by-case basis. About 70 per cent of Hungarian agricultural exports will receive gradual duty and levy reductions amounting to 60 per cent in 3 years. Exportable quantities will grow by 10 per cent pa for 5 years.

As regards EC exports of industrial goods to Hungary:

1. A 3-phase tariff reduction for goods subject to duties (about 90 per cent of EC industrial exports).

2. About 15 per cent of total imports were made duty-free in 3 years, ending at 1 January 1994.

3. The majority of goods will become duty-free until 1 January 2001, in 7 steps starting from 1995.

4. A non-vulnerable group will become duty-free starting from 1995.

Quantitative restrictions will be eliminated in all the above categories before the end of 2000.

As regards EC agricultural exports to Hungary, the country employs quantitative restrictions as the major trade policy tool in agricultural trade. Therefore, the main method of liberalising agricultural imports from the EC is a gradually increasing contingent within which import licences are automatically issued. It grows roughly by 5 per cent pa for 5 years, accompanied by a 10 per cent annual tariff reduction. In general,

Hungary has given about half as much in agricultural trade concessions as the EC.

Trade figures indicate that, at least until mid-1993, Hungary was not able to make full use of the new trade possibilities that have opened up. The new quotas and ceilings were not reached by Hungarian exporters.

TRADE WITH EFTA COUNTRIES

EFTA is traditionally a very important trading partner for Hungary. In the early-1990s about 15 per cent of exports were directed to EFTA countries, with over 20 per cent of imports coming from that region. Also, EFTA was the major source of the trade deficit both in 1991 and in 1992, with a US$652 million and US$796 million deficit with EFTA respectively.

The major trading countries are Austria and Switzerland, and they account for the majority of the deficit. The composition of EFTA trade is different from that with the EC. Raw materials play the major role in Hungarian exports, followed by machinery. This structure is characteristic of imports as well, indicating a relatively low degree of manufacturing co-operation between the partners. Trade with EFTA has been growing at a modest pace. While EC demand for Hungarian goods (except for food products) increased steadily in the early-1990s, that was not the case for EFTA. Imports from EFTA are dominated by steel and metallurgy goods, with manufacturing products taking second place. The share of chemicals and of light industry products is growing rapidly.

Hungary concluded a free trading agreement with EFTA in March 1993. It creates more favourable terms for Hungarian market access and may contribute to more balanced trade.

TRADE WITH FORMER COMECON

As earlier data indicated, Hungarian trade with Comecon suffered a major setback after 1989. Although it bounced back in 1992, one can still not see at what level it will stabilise. It is worth separating trade with the CIS from that with Eastern European countries for analysis.

Trade with the Soviet Union was a source of serious imbalances in the later years of the Comecon era. In general, it

Table 7.2   *Trade value index (previous years = 100), 1990–92*

Year	Currencies in which exports settled		Currencies in which imports settled	
	Convertible	Non-convertible	Convertible	Non-convertible
1990	115.5	73.7	111.5	79.5
1991	137.1	10.2	175.5	14.2
1992	107.3	0.1	99.8	4.4

Source: Kopint-Datorg.

was very lucrative for Hungarian firms to export to the USSR. It was an understanding market with practically no demand constraint in most export categories. Companies could exchange 'transferable' rouble income at a good (ie, unrealistically high) exchange rate. In addition, as opposed to dollar exports, roubles were converted to Hungarian currency, Forints, immediately after the delivery was made. That was very attractive from a cash flow point of view. It was no wonder that Hungarian companies accumulated a sizeable surplus worth over Rouble 1 billion by the late-1980s.

In 1990 Hungary opted for trade in hard currency with the Soviet Union alone among former Comecon countries. This situation put a strong constraint on trade, both parties being short of hard currency. The bilateral trade agreement between the two governments set forth trade in the value of US$1.7 billion Hungarian exports and US$2.1 billion Hungarian imports for 1991. In volume, this equalled about half the bilateral trade of the previous year. Reality has proved to be very different, and not much changed in 1992, despite the expansion of trade.

The Soviet Union took a 25 per cent share of Hungarian exports and supplied 22 per cent of its imports in 1989. These figures dropped to 13 per cent and 14 per cent respectively in 1992. There are many reasons behind this. Not only did the currency of trade change, but trading agents (the old massive state-owned, monopoly, specialised foreign trading firms) on both sides have largely disappeared. Earlier co-operation, working methods and long-term agreements collapsed and nothing much replaced them. The disintegration of the former USSR has made trade more costly (because individual republics have different rules), more risky and often less profitable. It should not be forgotten that most of the traditional trading partners have slid to technical or announced insolvency, as did many of the republics.

Trading intermediaries stepped in and they are responsible for much of the present volume of trade. Their contribution also means that goods initially exported to Western countries may end up in the CIS, which sheds suspicion on statistical figures indicating dramatic expansion of trade to advanced markets. It may help explain the expansion of Hungarian exports to the EC in 1990–92. Intermediaries have, on balance, played a positive role, taking over part of the risk, finance and marketing requirements of export deals.

Trade in the former USSR is still concentrated on machinery and agricultural produce on the export side, and raw materials and energy carriers on the import side. However, it is worth noting that imports of materials from the former Comecon area decreased by 5 per cent between 1991 to 1992, and that machinery imports increased by over 50 per cent. The most dynamic items on the export side were consumer goods and food products. The dependence of Hungary on energy imports from the CIS (mainly Russia) has not decreased much over the past few years.

The share of other Eastern European countries in trade also diminished markedly. The reasons are by and large the same as those already examined regarding the CIS. Very often these countries have similar export structures and their products compete in the medium to low price range in international markets. These prices sometimes are still high when quality is considered. The low price competitiveness and similar export structures result in a decline in their share of Hungarian trade. Some countries (eg Bulgaria) are now only marginal trading partners.

Hungary signed the Central European Free Trade Agreement (CEFTA) that sets forth practically free trade, and will reinstate the tariff conditions of trade of the Comecon years. Though this will certainly help market access, it is unlikely that the share of the region in Hungarian trade will recover to pre-1990 levels.

HUNGARY AND GATT

Hungary has been a member of GATT since 1973. The import liberalisation process that started in 1988 is a generally consistent programme, which puts Hungary among the countries with more liberal trade practice. As an open country heavily relying on foreign trade, Hungary advocates the lowest possible level of trade barriers and belonged to a group of countries seeking a liberal approach to international trade in the GATT Uruguay round. The successful completion of the Uruguay talks will ease market access conditions for Hungarian exports in many important markets. The liberal approach to trade in Hungary, however, may be modified as a result of growing trade balance problems – a phenomenon a number of experts and political decision makers attribute to too speedy a process of import liberalisation and leaving too little protection for domestic industrial and agricultural producers. A trade policy reversal is, however, unlikely in the near future.

Part II

The Business Infrastructure

8
Convertibility of the Forint

Creditanstalt-Bankverein

The policy of the National Bank of Hungary is aimed at the eventual restoration of forint convertibility, and this goal has been pursued with a degree of consistency since the mid-1980s. In fact, Hungary has fulfilled the most essential aspect of convertibility – the liberalisation of imports – for some time. In 1991, the range of imports with no licensing obligations was extended to cover more than 90 per cent of goods, which made the Hungarian forint practically convertible for current business transactions. The remaining limitations involve capital movements, private Hungarian individuals and tourist transactions. The achievement of full convertibility will be the result of a gradual process depending on the country's overall financial situation, and may be expected to take place within the next few years as the necessary preconditions are secured.

POLICY INGREDIENTS

The growing volume of international reserves, the decrease in the rate of inflation and the elimination of budget subsidies for price support contribute to establishing a more realistic exchange rate, and should be regarded as essential elements of the policy aiming for full convertibility. Important measures to create the appropriate economic environment included the establishment of financial infrastructure, involving essential legislation such as the Bank Act and the Central Bank Act of 1991 (liberating the National Bank from non-central bank functions). On the basis of these measures, the gradual liberalisation of currency regulations has taken place, with the most recent significant step being the establishment, from mid-1992, of the inter-bank foreign exchange market. This measure allows commercial banks to buy and sell foreign exchange without recourse to the National Bank.

The next move is expected to be the further liberalisation of currency regulations involving a new foreign exchange law. This legislation would loosen the remaining restrictions, although there would be no change in the obligation for businesses to offer their foreign exchange earnings for purchase by the National Bank of Hungary. (This obligation does not limit their free access to foreign exchange for business purposes.) The new law will liberalise the use of foreign currency for business travel and marketing expenses, and for the establishment and operation of representative offices abroad. Hungarian citizens are free to purchase unlimited foreign travel through travel agencies, but the currency limit for personal expenses remains in effect.

The new law will extend convertibility to foreign tourists, in as much as the full amount of exchanged currency will be reconvertible. Nevertheless, the free purchase by foreign citizens of convertible currencies for forints will not be possible. At present there are no restrictions on foreigners bringing capital into the country, their forint accounts can be used to purchase goods and services in Hungary and their capital and profits can be repatriated freely. Since 1992 foreigners have been able to keep a special kind of Hungarian forint account that can be used for trade transactions. According to the new law these account balances could also be used for equity investment.

THE EXCHANGE RATE

The exchange rate regime has undergone considerable changes in the past two decades. Until 1968, before the first round of economic reforms, Hungary had a multiple exchange rate system, under which separate exchange rates were maintained for different types of foreign currency transactions. This mechanism served to compensate for the impact of international price movements on domestic prices, neutralising changes in international commodity prices. In 1968, multiple exchange rates were replaced by a dual exchange rate system comprising a non-commercial rate and a commercial rate for all transactions, and these rates differed according to the partner's status as a Comecon member country or a Western industrialised country.

In 1981 the two exchange rates were unified and the rate against convertible currencies was based on a trade-weighted basket of 12 Western currencies. In December 1991 the composition of the basket was changed to the US dollar and the European Currency Unit (accounting for 50 per cent each). From August 1993, the ECU was replaced by the Deutschmark.

The government is trying to maintain realistic exchange rates, and prefers gradual adjustments to the large-scale devaluations that were common in 1991. Prior to 1990, a series of devaluations helped to establish confidence in the currency and the differential between the official and parallel exchange rates almost disappeared. It was the declared aim of this policy to minimise foreign exchange constraints by improving export price competitiveness through devaluations. However, higher than intended domestic inflation in the past two years encouraged the authorities to allow the forint to appreciate in real terms and, consequently, depreciation of the exchange rate failed to keep pace with the inflation differential between Hungary and its major trading partners. At present the pace of real appreciation is slowing compared with 1992, in line with a more balanced policy between the requirements of controlling inflation and facilitating adequate export growth (to the latter's favour).

Depreciation amounted to 20.8 per cent in 1991 and 5.4 per cent in 1992, relative to consumer price increases of 35 per cent and 23 per cent, respectively. (Industrial producer price increases were 32.6 per cent and 12.3 per cent, respectively, in these years.) Nominal depreciation continued in 1993, involving a 6.7 per cent devaluation in the first 6 months of the year and a 3 per cent depreciation in early July, while consumer price inflation was reported at 11.1 per cent for the period of January to June.

9

Banking and Financial Services

Creditanstalt-Bankverein

The Hungarian banking system has undergone a substantial transformation in the past six years. Banking reforms of a limited scope began in the early and mid-1980s when a handful of foreign banks were allowed into the Hungarian market. Prior to that the National Bank had a virtual monopoly of all central and commercial banking functions.

In 1987, a comprehensive banking reform was launched and a two-tier banking system established. Under the new system, the National Bank focuses on macroeconomic issues, such as monetary policy and exchange rate management, while the commercial banks deal with (*inter alia*) credit allocation, deposit collection, account settlement and payment transfers.

THE REFORM PROCESS

The Central Bank Act and the Bank Act, both of 1991, have contributed to the integration of Hungarian banking into the international financial system by the adoption of rules broadly in line with European standards. The Central Bank Act provides substantial autonomy to the National Bank. Although the bank's monopoly to raise foreign credits has been eliminated, such credits are still dependent on National Bank permission requirements. The Bank Act allows foreign investment in Hungarian banking, subject to government approval when the total foreign ownership exceeds 10 per cent of a bank's capital. There are also requirements to ensure adequate levels of capital and reserves in relation to business exposure, in harmony with international standards.

In 1987, by hiving off credit departments of the National Bank and transforming them into independent commercial banks, the three large commercial banks were established – the Hungarian Credit Bank (MHB), the Commercial Bank (OKHB) and the Budapest Bank. The number of new banks has since multiplied and currently the system consists of over 40 banks, of which more than 20 have been established with foreign participation.

Freedom of operations in the sector has been gradually broadened over the years. Initially, commercial banks were licensed to finance corporations and provide account settlement transactions, but were not permitted to keep deposits, carry out lending for private individuals or perform foreign exchange transactions. Since 1988, commercial banks have been licensed to carry out banking services for private individuals and, since 1990, have been providing a growing range of foreign currency services involving deposit collection and trade-related foreign currency transactions. An inter-bank foreign exchange market has been in operation since mid-1992.

The formation of the new banking system was largely completed by 1992. According to the Bank Act, four types of banks operate in Hungary:

- commercial banks offering essentially the full range of banking facilities;

- specialised financial institutions dealing with specific aspects of banking business;

- investment banks, which concentrate on the financing of long-term capital investment; and

- savings banks, which provide personal banking services.

In addition to banks, other institutions such as insurance companies, investment management firms and auditing firms have become an integral part of the financial system. In line with the Bank Act's stipulation that, following 1992, commercial banks would not be allowed to be members of the Budapest Stock Exchange (BSE), 50 brokerage firms have been established to handle business with the exchange. The BSE has been in operation since 1990.

In spite of government efforts to encourage diversification, the sector remains highly concentrated and the market's segmentation is considerable. The three large commercial banks together with the Foreign Trade Bank (MKB) and the State Savings Bank (OTP) represent 76 per cent of the banking market. State ownership in the sector is high, amounting to 66 per cent (ie 38 per cent direct and 28 per cent indirect ownership). Commercial banks mostly deal with corporate clients based on traditional client relationships dating back to the period before the 1987 reform, such as the Hungarian Credit Bank in the industry sector and the Commercial Bank for agriculture, while private customer service is dominated by a few banks including, traditionally, the State Savings Bank and, more recently, the Post Bank through its post office network. There is also an extensive country-wide network of savings co-operatives.

PROBLEM AREAS

Basic bottle-necks involve inadequate infrastructure and the lack of sufficiently experienced staff. While there has been definite improvement in these areas in the past two years, the deficiencies still result in slower bank transactions in Hungary than is customary in developed market economies.

The sector is faced with a growing demand for improvements to the scope, quality and speed of services, implying overall modernisation of infrastructure and the branch network, and the introduction of up-to-date procedures and systems. To cope with the challenge, important initiatives have been implemented or are under consideration in order to shore up efficiency in several ways. The bigger banks have introduced an impressive variety of savings products to broaden their funding base. Cash dispensers have appeared, and ATMs are in use, mostly in Budapest. Over 30 banks are linked up with SWIFT – more than in any other country in Central-East Europe.

A deposit insurance system has been set up, the first of its kind in the area, and an export guarantee institution has been established to support trade finance. Also, the Giro system starting in 1994 will provide faster handling of payment transfers. Nevertheless, further improvements and investment on a broad scale will be needed to deal with the shortcomings of the sector and to overcome the effect of decades of distortion.

Essentially, the sector's renewal is to be achieved within the framework of a substantial privatisation process, under which the government intends to improve ownership structures, strengthen the sector's financial position and improve technical know-how, possibly by the involvement of foreign capital. According to the Bank Act, state ownership of banks should fall to 25 per cent by January 1997 (except for OTP and the Post Bank which should stay 50 per cent and 20 per cent state owned, respectively).

Growth in the sector slowed in 1992 and its profitability declined. Loan business and profitability were hindered by the deteriorating creditworthiness of corporate borrowers, the increased number of bankruptcies and the strict provisioning requirements of the Bank Act regarding bad debts. In line with the shrinking number of creditworthy corporate debtors, bank lending to business decreased in real terms. Interest rates were high and credit was available mostly on a short-term basis. Three smaller banks went bankrupt in 1992 (the Entrepreneur Savings Co-operative was closed, while the General Bank of Venture Financing and Ybl Bank were saved by the West-deutsche Landesbank and Budapest Bank, respectively). While the damage caused by these minor bankruptcies was limited, they served as a reminder of the sector's vulnerability.

By the end of 1992, banks had accumulated a considerable stock of bad debts requiring outside intervention. (Doubtful and bad loans were reported at Ft 222 billion or 13.6 per cent in the latter half of 1992, compared to 7.1 per cent at the end of 1991.) According to the March 1993 credit consolidation agreement between the Ministry of Finance and commercial banks, bad loans of Ft 103 billion would be replaced by 20-year consolidation state bonds totalling Ft 79 billion. The bad loans in question are linked to about 4,500 mostly state-owned firms, of which 80 per cent relates to 200 companies.

The credit consolidation scheme is regarded as a temporary measure to strengthen banks' balance sheets in preparation for privatisation, and is expected to be complemented by another broadly similar package and other policies to directly support the banks' major debtors. At present, four principal state-owned banks are earmarked for privatisation. The Hungarian Foreign Trade Bank (MKB) and Budapest Bank, as the highest capitalised institutions among the large state-owned banks, are likely to be early candidates. Subsequently, privatisation of the

Commercial Bank (OKHB) and Hungarian Credit Bank (MHB) will take place in several stages.

THE STOCK EXCHANGE

The Budapest Stock Exchange was re-established in 1990, 40 years after its closure under the previous regime. Following an initial surge of activity, stock market turnover has declined reflecting the demise of the corporate sector and high interest rates. With less than 25 companies quoted at present, the number and value of transactions is quite small. Stock prices have generally fallen except for a few companies such as Styl, Fotex, Pick Salami and Danubius.

The bond market is showing signs of a modest revival. This market, which was established in Hungary in the 1980s, virtually collapsed in 1989. It is dominated by short-term government paper, though with inflation and interest rates declining the National Bank has started issuing fixed-rate bonds for longer maturities in order to stabilise the market. Corporate bond and commercial paper issues are becoming more common, dominated by multinational issuers backed by guarantees from their international parent company.

10

Privatisation

SJ Berwin & Co

THE MOVEMENT TOWARDS PRIVATISATION

Privatisation is central to Hungary's shift to a market economy. The trend towards privatisation began on 1 July 1990, when Hungary adopted legislation to effect the transformation of approximately 2200 state enterprises into corporate form and ultimately into private hands. Of these enterprises, 350 are large-scale business organisations employing up to 10,000 employees each with an annual turnover of Ft1–2 billion. Small and medium-sized enterprises number 600–700, employing up to 500 people, with a turnover of Ft5–200 million. Original government objectives envisaged a reduction in state ownership by 1994 to below 50 per cent. Certain strategic industries were to be exempt from privatisation and divided into 3 types of control – 100 per cent state ownership (eg utilities and munitions), 51 per cent state ownership (eg power and chemical companies) and 51 per cent national (state and private) ownership (eg the cement industry and certain commercial banks).

The State Property Agency (SPA) was created as a legal entity in 1990. It is managed by the government and is charged with holding the legal title to state property and promoting and supervising the privatisation process. SPA is authorised to sell the assets it controls to domestic or foreign national persons, business organisations (with or without legal personality) or private entrepreneurs. There was a lengthy and contentious political debate before the legislation was introduced (and indeed the debate still continues) as to whether privatisation ought to be allowed to proceed *ad hoc*, with state-owned enterprises devolving from central control as they find buyers, or whether an agency could be created to oversee the sell-off. The latter course was chosen to ensure that the change from public to private ownership was achieved in an orderly and controllable way.

However, there has been a gradual change in the perception of SPA since its creation. In 1990, state-owned enterprises were the initiators of the privatisation process, sometimes in partnership with a foreign investor. SPA had been set up merely to monitor the transaction value on behalf of the government. However, the managers of state enterprises were found to be ineffective in running state property and certain disadvantages were found in SPA being purely a reactive organisation that left the enterprises with the power to initiate the privatisation process. Therefore, there have been recent changes in the privatisation legislation, in particular the Sale Utilisation and Protection of Assets Temporarily Owned by the State Act (Act LIV of 1992 – 'the Privatisation Act') which provided SPA with additional powers to initiate privatisation. The Act also required state-owned enterprises to be transformed into joint stock companies by 30 June 1993. SPA therefore has stronger powers of management and the ability to focus on financial management.

To assist SPA, the Hungarian Investment and Development Company, a former investment bank, has been established. Furthermore, following the passing of the enabling Liquidation and Bankruptcy Act (Law IL of 1991) liquidations have proceeded and, although this can be seen as a form of privatisation, most of the value goes to the creditors.

Smaller firms

The Privatisation Act also contains provisions to enable the more speedy privatisation of some 800 smaller enterprises where the bureaucratic control of SPA is perceived as inhibiting the process. Therefore, a 'self-privatisation' programme using pre-qualified advisers (selected by way of tender) has been established to enable the sale of smaller enterprises. Essentially this will involve the advisers putting together a privatisation package which would effectively be 'rubber stamped' by SPA.

Furthermore, as an aid to progress on privatisation the Employees Part Ownership Programme Act (Act XLIV of 1992) has been passed which enables employees to acquire preferential ownership of shares in their employing company.

Other developments have seen the retention of 160 or so enterprises within state control. The Management and Utilisation of Permanent State Assets Act (Act LIII of 1992) creates a separate organisation (the Property Management Company Limited by Shares) which is responsible for the ongoing management of those assets which the government has decided, because of their strategic importance, will remain within state ownership.

Finally, it should also be noted that the dangers of restitution of property to those persons who can show they owned it prior to its expropriation by the state has been removed by the Compensation Act (Act XIV of 1991) which requires compensation rather than restitution for those persons who have had their property expropriated by the state. The Compensation Act should result in disputes about title to land no longer being an obstacle to privatisation.

THE LEGISLATION

There are several laws directly relevant to privatisation as follows:

- the Sale Utilisation and Protection of Assets Temporarily Owned by the State Act (Act LIV of 1992 – 'the Privatisation Act');

- the Management and Utilisation of Permanent State Assets Act (Act LIII of 1992); and

- the Small Shops and Restaurants Act (Act LXXIV of 1990).

Laws indirectly relevant to privatisation are as follows:

- the Enterprises Profit Tax Act (Acts IX and X of 1988);

- the Foreign Investment Act (Act XXIV of 1988);

- the Company Act (Act VI of 1988);

- the Securities Act (Act VI of 1990);

- the Compensation Act (Act XXV of 1992); and

- the Co-operatives Act (Acts I and II of 1992).

ROLE OF SPA

SPA exercises ownership rights on behalf of the state in respect of the assets of state-owned enterprises, the assets of subsidiaries of a state-owned enterprise, the shares of state-owned companies transformed into companies under the terms of the earlier Transformation Act (Act XIII of 1989) which have not been acquired by a third party and other shares which are held directly in a transformed company but belonged to SPA at the time the Privatisation Act came into force. Excluded from SPA's ownership are assets to be permanently held by the state in accordance with the Management and Utilisation of Permanent State Assets Act (Act LIII of 1992), Treasury assets excluded by special Acts, assets previously transferred but which have become the property of local authorities and the assets of the National Bank of Hungary.

In exercising its rights of ownership on behalf of the government, SPA is directed by the government through ministers responsible for privatisation. SPA may also be charged with such other tasks as the government may decide.

SPA is administered by a board of directors consisting of 11 members. The decisions of the board are binding on the managing director of SPA. Prior to board decisions, the chairman of the board may ask the minister responsible for privatisation for the government's opinion on a particular matter. The chairman and members of the board of SPA are appointed by the Prime Minister for four years. Members of the board of SPA are disqualified from being employees of SPA or the State Property Management Company Limited by Shares (the organisation responsible for supervising those assets which remain within the permanent ownership of the state). They are also disqualified from being a member of the supervisory board of a company managing assets belonging to SPA or from occupying a senior position in a finance institution or other organisation concerned with the sale of securities. SPA is managed by a managing director and must act within the framework of the Asset Management Policy Guidelines adopted annually by parliament. These guidelines determine the tasks of the SPA, and compliance with them, publicity, competitiveness and realistic asset valuations are the major issues of the privatisation process as far as SPA is concerned.

SPA is charged with protecting the property of existing state enterprises prior to their transformation. In the case of transactions exceeding a certain value, SPA is authorised to approve such transactions because they may have a definite effect on the viability of their own privatisation. The following activities of state enterprises fall under SPA's scrutiny:

- relinquishing a contribution in kind to a contributor where the contribution is in excess of 10 per cent of the value of the enterprise or amounts to at least Ft20 million;

- disposal of real estate, including leasing contracts, to a value in excess of Ft20 million;

- disposal of any other asset of the enterprise, including leasing contracts, in excess of 30 per cent of the value of the enterprise or Ft50 million; and

- any other contracts, including leasing contracts, which have the effect of allowing some other person to take more than a 50 per cent interest in the enterprise.

These rules do not apply to contracts entered into in the normal course of business, contracts concluded with another state enterprise or contracts concluded with the State Treasury.

In approving (or otherwise) the contract, SPA may:

- if it considers the valuation to be unsafe, order a further valuation and, if the valuation exceeds the original by at least 30 per cent, then the cost of the valuation is charged to the enterprise; or

- if it considers that market conditions warrant it, prescribe a disposal by way of tender; or

- attach conditions to the disposal or refuse to approve the contract if the enterprise fails to fulfill SPA's conditions by the deadline, or if the sale is contrary to the interests of the state.

THE PRIVATISATION PROCESS

As indicated previously, the aim of the government as enshrined in the Privatisation Act was for all state enterprises to be transformed by 30 June 1993. To facilitate this aim the Act sets down two procedures, one applicable to enterprises with a transformation plan in place by 30 June 1993 or where the enterprise is a small enterprise privatised under the supervision of an appointed expert, and the other for those enterprises which have failed to put in place a transformation plan by 30 June 1993. There are, however, several general rules which are applicable to all privatisations. The so-called founders' rights in the enterprise are exercised by SPA. This gives SPA real control of the initiation of the privatisation process.

Companies to be transformed must prepare a transformation plan and a draft balance sheet. The transformation plan must include the following information:

- a business plan;
- an inventory of assets;
- draft articles of association of the new company;
- a declaration of intention by the new members;
- an employment and social plan;
- an environmental statement;
- a statement as to how the shares are to be allotted to employees; and
- a statement of potential for hive-off of businesses which can be operated independently.

The balance sheet must be approved by either the auditor or, if the company is to have one, the supervisory board.

The provisions of the Company Act (Act IV of 1988) apply to the company during the transformation process and the company must publish a decision to transform in the official company gazette which must include an outline of the transformation plan and the draft balance sheet.

Once transformed, the new company is the effective successor of the state enterprise. As such therefore, the new company possesses the rights but is also subject to the obligations of the state enterprise, and is bound by existing collective agreements with employees. The new company does not have any new or special tax liabilities arising from the transformation process, but any tax allowance due to a state enterprise will be carried forward to the new company. The new company is also entitled to the benefit of all official permits issued to the state enterprise prior to transformation, but the new company is only entitled to continue with a concession so long as the government possesses a majority share in the company.

Upon transformation, private investors may acquire all or part of the equity capital. Until private investors acquire the capital the shares remain within SPA's ownership and SPA undertakes the management of the company. Also on transformation, the local authority where the company's property is situated is entitled either to compensation based on the value of the land upon which the business is situated or alternatively to be offered shares in the company equivalent to that value.

Certain company law rules are waived on transformation. For example, the requirements of the Company Act for minimum paid-up capital for certain companies are waived; a limited liability company must have a supervisory board until the end of the first year of operation even if it is not required to do so by the Company Act; and creditors in the former state enterprise may waive payment of debts due in return for an allotment of shares on the same basis as if the creditor had made a contribution of capital in kind.

Transformation plan in place

As indicated previously, the Act differentiates between those state enterprises which have a transformation plan in place prior to 30 June 1993 and those which do not. Where there is a transformation plan in place by 30 June 1993 any of three procedures can be followed: transformation under the guidance of SPA; transformation initiated by a state enterprise; and the so-called simplified transformation procedure currently only applicable to small enterprises.

Transformation under the guidance of SPA is applicable to those state enterprises under the direct control of the state (as opposed to being self-managed). Transformation of state-controlled enterprises can be initiated either by the enterprise or by SPA. In addition, SPA has the power to convert the state-controlled enterprise into a self-managed enterprise or it may appoint a company commissioner to prepare the transformation of the state-controlled enterprise. The company commissioner manages the enterprise in accordance with direct instructions from SPA. Once the commissioner has been appointed, the manager of the state-controlled company is relieved of his duties.

Self-managed enterprises can decide to privatise by a vote to that effect passed by two-thirds of the enterprise council at a general meeting of the employees. Where such a decision is taken the draft transformation plan and balance sheet is presented to SPA. The enterprise council or general meeting as applicable must inform its employees of the general principles of the transformation plan – particularly the effects upon their conditions of employment – and this must be done at least 30 days prior to notification to SPA of the intention to privatise. Confirmation that this has been done must also be communicated to SPA. Until SPA has considered the documents submitted to it, the enterprise may not commit itself to a form of legal agreement. SPA must agree or veto the terms and conditions of the draft plan within 30 days of the original notification by the enterprise. SPA can extend this time limit by a further 30 days. The enterprise must adhere to directions as to any method of sale given by SPA.

The so-called simplified privatisation procedure applies to the sale of those companies as directed by SPA and so far has been limited to smaller enterprises. The privatisation process is undertaken under the supervision of an expert selected by competitive tender from a list of retained experts. The expert is given the same powers as SPA in that he may conclude a contract with the purpose of transforming the state enterprise into a company and, on a subsequent sale, may exercise (on behalf of SPA) the rights of ownership in the shares of the new company. The expert may also dispose of the shares in the company as agent for SPA, and in the same way permitted by it. SPA may attach conditions to restrict the activities of the expert and decides on his remuneration. The expert owes a duty of care to SPA and is responsible to it in discharging his functions.

Enterprises which failed to commence transformation by 30 June 1993 must prepare the articles of association for the company and must have convened the inaugural meeting of the company by 31 December 1993. The provisions of the Company Act apply to companies transformed in this way. However, such enterprises do not prepare the transformation plan although they are obliged to compile an inventory of the enterprise's assets. Following transformation, the board of directors of the company is appointed by SPA, save for those directors appointed by the supervisory board of the employees in accordance with the Company Act.

Until it is disposed of, SPA is responsible for the management of all state property under its control, but it may appoint a manager to discharge its duties. SPA must dispose of state property in accordance with the Asset Management Policy Guidelines approved annually by parliament. SPA may give the manager of the property the power to sell it, but the property must be disposed of in the same way as it would have been by SPA. Also, SPA and/or the manager, as applicable, must consult the affected employees at least 30 days prior to the decision to sell the state property, outlining to them the consequences of a sale on their conditions of employment.

Disposal procedures

The disposal of state property initiated by SPA is generally either by way of a public placing of shares in accordance with the Company Act or by competitive tender following the rules of competition procedure contained in the Privatisation Act. In evaluating tenders SPA and/or the manager must take into account the terms of each tender that relate to conditions of employment of the employees and proposals for reducing environmental damage. Where tenders are equal, preferential treatment is given to management buy-outs backed by at least 25 per cent of employees and participants in the employees' part ownership programme (see below). The results of the tender process must be published in daily newspapers.

In cases where SPA finds it difficult to dispose of shares in a transformed enterprise, it may dispose of them on a 'leased basis' pursuant to which the 'lessee' provides services to the company over a period of time and, following expiration of the 'lease', the lessee becomes the absolute owner of the shares. Such an arrangement may only take place following a competitive tender. The duration of the lease cannot be longer than 10 years. During the period of the lease the lessee is entitled to all membership rights except for the right to sell the shares.

If market conditions are unfavourable to the disposal of state property, then SPA may manage the property in the interim. However, it is specifically stated in the Privatisation Act that SPA is only entitled to manage property in exceptional circumstances and for temporary periods. Ministerial approval is necessary for the continuing management of the property.

The government has decided that certain strategic assets

should remain in permanent state ownership, and it has passed the Management and Utilisation of Assets Permanently Remaining in State Ownership Act (Act LIII of 1992). Such assets may be included within permanent state ownership if:

- justified by economic–strategic, national economy or other important interests;

- the property or part of the property serves national public service purposes and can only be economically operated by a unified system of research or production;

- the preparation of the property for sale would take a particularly long time.

Such property will be transferred into a so-called State Property Company Limited by Shares ('the Management Company') specifically established by the Act. The shares in the Management Company are exclusively owned by the state. The Management Company is responsible for the transformation of the state enterprise into a company and the rights of ownership of its shares remain with the management company. Shareholders' rights in the management company are exercised by the relevant minister. The Management Company is managed by a board of directors consisting of 11 members and there is a supervisory board consisting of 5–7 members. The Management Company must retain the status quo of its ownership in companies in which it holds shares – ie if it owns 100 per cent it may not sell any shares and if it owns 51 per cent it must retain that majority. As with SPA, the Management Company is empowered to appoint a private sector manager to manage the state property on its behalf.

The Employees Part Ownership Programme Act (Act XLIV of 1992) was enacted to accelerate privatisation and to provide for a means by which employees may acquire shares. This is achieved by a legal entity, the employees' part ownership programme ('the EPP'), which acquires shares beneficially on behalf of employees. There are certain conditions which must be fulfilled by employees in order to be able to participate in the programme, and the EPP must be established by at least 25 per cent of the employees. The EPP, once established, has a constitution and decision making lies between the general meeting of the employees and the board of management.

The Small Shops and Restaurants Act (Act LXXIV of 1990)

contains the privatisation process for the sale by tender to the private sector of small shops and restaurants. However, this Act is not of particular interest to Western investors because these small businesses have been reserved for Hungarian nationals as part of the government's drive to establish an entrepreneurial class.

Finally, the passing of the Co-operative Acts (Acts I and II of 1992), apart from setting up a new code regulating the establishment and management of co-operatives, permits transformation of co-operatives to limited liability companies or joint stock companies following agreement of a two-thirds majority of members of the co-operative. The prerequisite for the transformation is a distribution of all of the assets of the co-operative among its members, who have a choice either to become a member of the newly transformed co-operative by seeking shares in the new company or to carry on the business themselves.

11

Restructuring State Enterprises

KPMG Peat Marwick

To Hungarians, as to their neighbours, the collapse of communism meant the promise of consumer goods, capital, technology,
know-how and, in other words, prosperity. The transformation of
a command economy – with each transaction part of an intricate
web of artificial relationships – into a market economy calls for a
new approach to property, with clear definition of ownership and
responsibility. This is not a process that can be decreed overnight
as nationalisation and state confiscation were. A new class of
entrepreneurs must be grown and foreign investment is essential.

Speed in privatising companies is one of the standard
measurements of success of the privatisation programmes in
Central and Eastern Europe. Observers watch with awe mixed
with admiration the efforts made in the Czech Republic in its
massive off-loading of state-owned assets of dubious or unknown
value on to its unsuspecting citizenry. The Hungarians have
shunned such populist undertakings. But with all the arguments
concerning the speed of privatisation and the regulatory framework, it is not surprising that there is little consensus on how to
restructure, or whether restructuring should be the cart or the
horse in the process.

The privatisation process itself seems to suffer from muddled
thinking: should it raise revenue or should it create clear
ownership and responsibility boundaries and regulations essential for the working of a free market economy? Is restructuring
more effective in the long term with companies split up and sold
as separate units rather than as a whole? There is no blueprint

for action. Restructuring is a slow process and, in all probability, too slow for a government with thousands of companies on its books. The Privatisation Act, although acknowledging that not all companies can be sold immediately, does not address restructuring. The idea behind some of the early flotations on the Budapest Stock Exchange (BSE), such as Ibusz, seems to have been that even though the companies could not swim, they would eventually float their way out of trouble.

The State Property Agency (SPA) was assigned the task of representing state interests in approximately 90 per cent of state-owned companies, as well as privatising them. The SPA was torn between these main responsibilities. In the autumn of 1992, State Asset Holding Company (AVRt) Ltd was created to take over from the SPA ownership of those companies in which the State expected to maintain a degree of ownership. The portfolio taken over comprised about 160 of the country's largest companies and banks. The AVRt is responsible for privatising shares in these companies up to the statutory limit. Companies to be 100 per cent privatised remain with the SPA.

COMPANY NEEDS

So far the process has only touched upon a fraction of companies and there are many large groups losing money. Reforms in 1968 allowed Hungarian companies relative but limited independence. Enterprises were allowed to set prices and wages but within the strict limits of the instructions set in 'the Plan' and other informal arrangements such as guidelines and indicators emanating from the authorities. The other point of the reform was that enterprises continued to be sheltered from the world economy as they carried on exporting and importing through specialised foreign trade organisations. Revitalising industry will be a hard struggle. Hungarian companies share common features with their East European counterparts. They are often:

- highly diversified;
- highly vertically integrated;
- heavily indebted; and
- overmanned.

Enterprises were organised to perform only the production

function of a Western company – the marketing and strategy functions and skills were largely absent. There was relatively little contact with customers and product end-users in the domestic market. Many enterprises are large lumbering monopolies which need to be split up into competitive units leaving non-essential assets to be liquidated. Traditionally, they produced a broad range of goods which resulted in lack of focus. They would also produce their own tools, components and spare parts. Service functions such as R&D, catering, maintenance and repairs are done in-house. Managers of state enterprises also suffered from the absence of useful management information because financial accounting systems were designed to meet the requirements of the tax authorities.

To continue operations most will need to secure funding and to restructure their debts. However, the long-term survival of companies means more than the initial injection of cash. It involves assessing medium to long-term strategy. A company's ability to survive will depend on a number of factors, such as:

- its financial condition;

- its competitive position;

- opportunities for asset disposal;

- possibilities for cost reduction;

- management organisation; and

- the labour force.

Many companies are viable. They present opportunities for radical increases in productivity, reduction in overheads and inventory, of improvements in quality, and in the use of assets and management information systems. Tungsram is a case in point. The company, one of the few with a solid international reputation in its sector, was acquired in 1989 by General Electric of the US. The number of employees was cut from 18,000 to 10,200, productivity and sales have risen, peripheral businesses were sold off, the company hierarchy was flattened, and the turnaround time between order and delivery was halved. Still the future of the company is clouded by three years of losses.

Companies are having to adapt at a time of considerable economic uncertainty. Macroeconomic reforms have resulted in a widespread fall in domestic demand. Traditional markets have shrunk due to the collapse of the Soviet Union. Output has declined dramatically. The passing of time weighs heavily on state-owned companies. With the privatisation process so sluggish, their financial condition continues to deteriorate and their value drops, which in turn makes it harder to find a foreign investor. High interest rates means borrowing for restructuring is out of the question. Even borrowing for short-term working capital is difficult to find.

PRIVATISATION AND RESTRUCTURING

The efforts of SPA have met with mixed results. When Hungary started its privatisation programme, it was burdened with a heavy legacy of debt from the communist regime. It sought out the highest price possible for the companies it sold. Foreigners could pay more and represent 80 per cent of the revenues to date. Raising hard currency is an important element of privatisation. Of the privatisation revenues obtained in 1992, Ft30 billion went straight into the state budget, Ft6.5 billion was used to meet obligations on the Hungarian state debt, Ft1.6 billion went to local councils, Ft2.7 billion went to the social security fund, and only Ft500 million was earmarked for investment and restructuring. The early privatisation candidates were drawn from the relatively successful and attractive enterprises. Increasingly, the candidates will become less attractive and more difficult to sell.

Unlike the German Treuhandanstalt, SPA does not support companies or investors financially to facilitate the transfer of ownership into private hands. The majority of privatisations so far have involved trade sales where a private sector buyer, usually a foreigner, becomes involved in the management of the newly privatised company. The winner is the highest bidder irrespective of the perceived needs of the company. However, a trade sale is a secure way of bringing in capital and sound management skills and restructuring should be left to the new owners. If investments are carried out before the sale, these may not meet the precise needs of the buyer, and the sale price may therefore not reflect the full value of the investment.

Companies involved in public flotation, management buy-outs, or employee share ownership programmes where the management remains the same, may not have the resources to restructure. Employee share ownership may actually limit the management's ability to improve productivity through redundancies. If the company is privatised unrestructured, the hope is that the harsh discipline of the market will force companies to restructure, because of the threat of bankruptcy, the threat of takeovers and shareholder pressure for improved performance.

New methods are being experimented with which involve the breaking up of companies and leasing their assets, with an option to buy at a later stage. But such a method is still perceived as a last resort solution and will be applied only when a cash sale has failed to materialise. For SPA, this involves taking a risk on the creditworthiness of the new owners and a loss of revenue because lease payments are paid out of profits before tax. The lessees exercising their option to buy in a few years' time will have established a track record and should find it easier to convince bankers to back expansion.

In the meantime, those companies for which privatisation is not an immediate prospect, without radical restructuring, may sink into bankruptcy. The social consequences are obvious. There are good reasons why the state does not want to undertake a politically sensitive job – liquidating subsidiaries or plant might go against public opinion.

BANKRUPTCY

Hungary's Bankruptcy Act which came into force on 1 January 1992 made it possible for creditors to force companies into bankruptcy if they did not pay their bills within 90 days. This removed the prop from several thousand companies that continued to buy goods without paying for them.

Bankrupt companies are bringing down successful private companies. The first listed casualty of the bankruptcy legislation was Terraholding, an international trading company which was quoted on the BSE. The Cabinet has started debating amendments to bankruptcy legislation in order to stall what has been perceived as an unnecessarily large number of potential liquidations. However, bankruptcies are not all as bad as they seem. Bankruptcies and liquidations may enable the privatisation process to gather speed as it will simplify the disposal of unwieldy structures, enabling them to be broken down into their more attractive parts.

BANK RESTRUCTURING

The government has initiated a clean up of the balance sheets of state-owned banks which is viewed as an essential component of the bank privatisation process. The four state banks have been making provisions against dubious debts during the course of 1992 in an attempt to abide by the requirements of the new Bank Act requiring them to reach a capital asset ratio of 8 per cent. Provision against non-performing assets is tax deductible. Due to the wave of bankruptcies, the banks have had to make provisions at an even faster pace than was originally envisaged when the banking legislation was adopted.

RESTRUCTURING AND THE FOREIGN INVESTOR

Many Western companies underestimate the time and costs involved in trying to turn a company around. The costs of selling off non-core businesses may outweigh the cash benefits – debt write-offs of old debts which had accumulated on the balance sheet for years and increased borrowing costs may well cancel out any increase in productivity.

12

Foreign Investment

SJ Berwin & Co

The combination of a number of different laws has made the Hungarian market more attractive to foreign investors. First, Act VI of 1988 on Business Societies, Associations, Companies and Ventures ('the Company Act') establishes the framework for private enterprise. Secondly, the Act for the Transformation of State Enterprises (Act XIII of 1989 – 'the Transformation Act') initially promoted the privatisation of state enterprises, but this has now been replaced by the Sale Utilisation and Protection of Assets Temporarily Owned by the State Act (Act LIV of 1992 – 'the Privatisation Act'). Thirdly, the Foreign Investment Act (Act XXIV of 1988 as amended by Act XCVIII of 1990) contains provisions enabling and encouraging foreign investors to form joint ventures and to establish Hungarian business associations (including wholly-owned entities). The aim of this chapter is to give an overview of foreign investment generally, as permitted and encouraged by the Foreign Investment Act ('the FIA').

GENERAL PROVISIONS

The FIA uses the collective term 'business association with foreign participation'. It includes all business associations that are owned in part or exclusively by a foreigner. It is also irrelevant whether the foreigner is already a member of the business association at the time of its establishment or whether he joins the business association subsequently when it is in operation.

A business association as defined by the FIA has a wider meaning than a limited liability or joint stock company. It is an entity (whether corporated or unincorporated) formed for the purpose of carrying on a commercial activity. However, for ease, business associations will be referred to throughout this chapter as 'BAs' and business associations with foreign participation as 'BAFPs'.

In order for the provisions of the FIA to apply, two conditions need to be fulfilled. First, the person participating in the BA must be a foreigner. A foreigner for the purposes of the FIA is some person or entity who is treated as a foreigner for the purposes of the foreign exchange regulations. The foreign exchange regulations state that a foreigner is a foreign national or a legal entity formed in accordance with a foreign system of law. Secondly, the BA should have its registered address in Hungary. The FIA does not extend to BAs which have a plant or branch in Hungary but have their registered address abroad. The FIA also does not apply to a subsidiary of a BAFP (the subsidiary is treated as a wholly domestic BA).

THE PROTECTION OF FOREIGN INVESTMENT

The FIA states that all foreign investments are fully protected. Investors are indemnified by the Hungarian state against losses resulting from nationalisation or expropriation of their property, or any similar eventuality. The right of indemnification may be enforced in the courts against the state authority which authorised the expropriation of the property. The value of the claim would be for the actual value of the investment and is payable in the currency in which it was originally made. Actual value is not defined in the FIA, nor is there any formula for its calculation. The compensation is payable by the administrative agency responsible for the loss. Following a decision of the Constitutional Court in 1990, any decision of any state administrative agency may be challenged before the courts.

The fundamental issue for a foreigner contemplating an investment in Hungary is a guarantee that profit from the investment can be provided in convertible currency and invested capital can be freely taken out of the country. The FIA states that a foreign participator in a BA may exchange at the official exchange rate into the currency of investment:

- his share of the profit of the BA;
- any cash contribution returned to him as a result of a decrease in authorised capital;

- his share in the assets in the case of a winding up of the BA; and

- the sale proceeds derived from the sale of his interest.

These monies may be transferred to another country without the need for any licence or permit from the foreign exchange authority. The foreigner may only exercise these rights if the BA has the necessary amounts in forints at its disposal. These rights of repatriation are not restricted to investors but also extend to managers, members of the supervisory board and employees. These persons have the right to transfer 50 per cent of their after-tax earnings to another country in the currency of their country of permanent residence.

The provisions of the FIA may only be applied where they are not inconsistent with obligations under international treaties. Thus, for example, bilateral or multilateral agreements or double taxation treatment will take precedence.

A further scheme of protection exists for British investors in the form of the Bilateral Investment Promotion and Protection Agreement entered into between the United Kingdom and Hungary in 1987, which came into force in August 1987. The agreement caters for the protection of present and future investments from expropriation by ensuring the payment of compensation, and provides for the settlement of investment disputes, the transfer of profits and the repatriation of capital. Notably, the agreement also provides for international arbitration in the event of disputes between investors and the Hungarian Republic, and between the Hungarian Republic and the United Kingdom.

ESTABLISHMENT OF A BAFP

Most of the more stringent requirements imposed upon BAFPs over and above those imposed upon domestic BAs have been repealed. The procedure has therefore become simpler. Since the start of 1990, a foreigner is no longer required to show that he qualified as a firm/BA under his own domestic law. Furthermore, since the start of 1991 no licence from the Hungarian government is required to acquire a majority interest in a Hungarian BA. The legal recognition of a BAFP may not be refused due to expediency or business or political considerations.

The registration of the BA in the trade register may only be refused by the Court of Register if the articles of association (or foundation deed) are contrary to mandatory statutory provisions.

There are certain rules contained in the FIA governing foreign participation in a company which are unique to that participation. Where the foreign party makes a contribution in cash, it must be made in a convertible currency, although this provision may be excluded by international agreement. Therefore, if a bilateral or multilateral international agreement has different and inconsistent provisions these will prevail over the FIA. There is a further exception where the foreign investor waives the repatriation of his profits and instead uses the profits either to increase the capital of the BA or to invest in a new BA. Similar benefits apply where the foreigner uses sale proceeds from his investment in establishing a new BA with a registered office in Hungary.

Contributions may be made 'in kind' rather than in cash. There is no distinction between foreigner and resident contributions in kind. The permitted categories of in kind contributions are tangible assets, negotiable assets with real value and any intellectual property or other valuable right. However, the distinction between foreigner and resident with regard to in kind contributions does become important in view of customs duties and taxation.

Means of production supplied by a foreign participator as a contribution in kind are exempt from customs duty. However, if the foreign participator is resident in Hungary he is not entitled to this benefit by importing the means of production. Means of production are defined in the FIA as machines, equipment or appliances and other vehicles necessary for the production of goods and for their transportation, or for providing services as part of the regular business activities of the BA. The FIA differentiates between in kind contributions imported for production or trade. If the BA sells or leases the means of production within three years of it being supplied the customs duty must be repaid.

Foreigners can only acquire registered shares, as opposed to bearer shares. Where bearer shares are to be sold to foreigners they must be converted into registered shares. Where a foreigner inherits bearer shares they must be converted into registered shares within one year of registration.

If the proposed registered capital of a joint stock company is oversubscribed and therefore subscriptions may be rejected in accordance with the Company Act, then if the company is a BAFP the subscription by the state or state financial institution may also be rejected.

BAFP OPERATIONS

The BAFP is generally to be considered as a domestic BA. Therefore, unless otherwise provided in the FIA, the legislation governing domestic BAs also applies to BAFPs.

Hungarian commercial laws generally apply equally to companies with foreign participation and to wholly-owned, domestic entities, including specifically the laws relating to:

- prices;
- accounting;
- the quality of goods and services;
- competition; and
- insolvency.

Within this framework, BAFPs are entirely free to enter into contracts for the same purposes and in the same way as wholly Hungarian-owned corporations. This is beneficial for the foreign investor because the BA established by him or operating with his participation may exercise rights which may not be directly exercised by foreigners themselves.

Where companies with foreign participation undertake transactions involving foreign currencies or foreign exchange the rules that apply are the same as those that control transactions entered into by domestic BAs. The BAFP securing a loan from abroad is in the same position as a domestic BA in that it requires the permission of the appropriate Hungarian authorities. Generally, BAFPs are subject to the same regulations in relation to their assets as domestic BAs in that they may deal freely with their assets according to Hungarian law and their articles of association (or founders' deed).

A BAFP (as opposed to the foreign party itself) is allowed to acquire real property where it is necessary for the conduct of the business of the company as laid down in the articles of association (or founders' deed). The extent of this provision is unclear but it would appear that speculative land acquisition is not permitted. A foreign person may acquire real property with the permission of the Ministry of Finance provided:

- it does not violate the interests of the Hungarian state, or local authority, tourist, cultural, social welfare or other social interests; or

- the foreigner's real estate in Hungary has been appropriated; or

- the foreigner exchanges certain real estate in Hungary for other real estate in Hungary; or

- the reason for acquisition is to eliminate joint ownership.

However, there are occasions when the BAFP is subject to different provisions than those that apply to domestic BAs. For example, unless other legislation provides otherwise, provisions of a non-civil nature addressed to state economic organisations or co-operatives do not apply to the BAFP

The law regulating employer/employee relations is explained in Chapter 17. However, it is expressly provided in the FIA that BAFPs must pay their employees' social insurance contributions, that the Hungarian Labour Code is binding on them, and that social security payments are only payable in relation to those foreign employees who wish to take advantage of the free Hungarian medical and social insurance services. This latter qualification also applies to the National Pension Fund. The rules governing the upper limits of remuneration (ie if wages are raised in excess of a predetermined limit then this will be taken into account in the BA's profit and tax) only apply to BAFPs if the interest of foreigners is less than 20 per cent of Ft5 million. Executives, managers and members of the supervisory board of a joint stock company may be foreigners although it is not made clear what proportion must be Hungarian.

BAFPs, as with domestic BAs, must keep their books in Hungarian forints and, with the exception of duty-free zone companies, must express their balance sheet in Hungarian forints. However, BAFPs can account for a cash contribution by foreign participants made in convertible currency in the currency of contribution. This does not require permission from the foreign exchange authority. Such foreign currency may be used for purchasing means of production, but the BAFP does not have the right to pay in foreign currency if payment is due in forints.

CUSTOMS-FREE ZONES

A foreign party may establish, participate in or invest in a BA established in a customs-free zone. These zones have been created in 7 of Hungary's 19 counties and are intended to assist in regional development. Customs-free zone BAs are not a separate form of BA and the general Company Act is equally applicable to them. However, there is an additional requirement in that the Ministry of Finance must have declared the area where the BA intends to locate as a customs-free zone. Customs-free zones are considered as foreign territory for the application of customs procedure, foreign exchange and foreign trade rules.

The characteristic features of such BAs are:

- The BA may keep its books in convertible currency and may prepare its balance sheet on a foreign currency basis.

- The BA conducts its business in convertible currency and may keep necessary amounts up to the limit of its authorised capital with a domestic bank. Amounts in excess of this may be kept in any financial institution. Everyday payments may therefore be made in forints purchased from an Hungarian financial institution.

- The BA may obtain loans from both domestic and foreign persons without obtaining permission of the foreign exchange authority.

- The rules relating to price regulation and supervision by the state do not apply.

Licences to operate in these zones are obtained from the Minister of Finance.

ESTABLISHING AN OPERATIONAL BASE

Establishing a place of business in Hungary is dependent upon the intended method of operation in the country. The mechanics of purchasing premises are dealt with in the Civil Code and will be explained in Chapter 15. The ways in which joint ventures may be created with Hungarian entities, the means by which foreigners may form BAs and the methods by which they are able to acquire shares in existing economic corporations are governed by the Company Act and are explained in Part III of this book.

Decree 3/89 of the Ministry of International Economic Relations (the Ministry of Trade) on the Business Representation of Foreigners and their Information and Service Offices provides that foreign investors can either commission an Hungarian agent to act on their behalf in Hungary or establish a representative office in their own right. Where a resident Hungarian national is appointed as representative to undertake regular enterprise activities as the foreign company's agent, a foreign trade contract (the meaning of this term is explained later in the chapter) must be completed between the parties.

A representative office may be established for the purpose of carrying on business in Hungary. It will be registered as a foreign business by the Ministry of International Economic Relations and at the Court of Registration. Registration can be refused where it is considered that the registration of the foreign entity would hinder the creation of Hungarian businesses with the same goals as the foreign entity. The representative office may be set up for the following purposes:

- the preparation, negotiation and conclusion of contracts between the foreign entity and Hungarian parties;

- the operation of warehousing facilities and providing customer services and after-sales services;

- organising publicity and information; and

- the representation of the foreign entity in third party states.

The FIA and the Company Act do not apply to representations.

Alternatively, the office may be a simple information office established using the same procedure as a representative office. In such a case it is not able to carry on commercial activities but it can conduct servicing, marketing and information functions on behalf of the foreign entity. (The distinction between a representative and information office has important fiscal consequences.)

FOREIGN TRADE

The Minister of International Economic Relations controls access to foreign trade. The regulations governing foreign trade relate specifically to the formation of foreign trade contracts. A foreign trade contract is a contract concluded between an Hungarian individual and a foreign person in relation to certain defined activities as set out in the Foreign Trade Act (Act III of 1974 as amended). All Hungarian companies have the right to conduct foreign trade provided they have been registered in the register maintained by the Ministry. A company must be included in the register if it fulfils the organisational and personnel requirements laid down by the Ministry. Once this permission has been granted, the new status is recorded in the company register. All such contracts must be in writing.

The trade activities of foreigners within Hungary are also under the control of the Minister for International Economic Relations. This is the case even if the foreign party is operating through a representative office within Hungary. However, in these circumstances, the foreign party is able to trade (on a temporary basis) with Hungarian parties in possession of foreign trade licences, without having such a licence himself. Otherwise, a licence from the Minister is always needed by a foreigner. All the usual penalties under civil and criminal law apply to anyone acting in contravention of these regulations.

Since 1 January 1990, a licence has not always been necessary for certain imports and exports unless licences are specifically required by legislation for those products.

The parties to an agreement involving foreign trade may agree on the law to govern relations between them, and that any dispute between them can be resolved by arbitration. While the Hungarian party will often naturally prefer the operation of Hungarian law, the practice is growing for the use of neutral systems of law and arbitration. The laws of Switzerland are frequently chosen, and arbitration under the rules of the International Court of Arbitration of the International Chamber of Commerce and the Zurich Chamber of Commerce are also increasingly popular.

13

Accounting and Valuation

KPMG Peat Marwick

THE ACCOUNTING SYSTEM

In the past, tax regulations and economic planning were the major influences on accounting regulations. Accounting was one element in the information system designed to help state planners allocate resources. The collection of financial data was fundamentally designed with the production of national statistics in mind. Government agencies used this information to control production in quantitative terms. Comparability was ensured by a uniform chart of accounts supported by detailed regulations on bookkeeping and the preparation of financial statements. Assets and liabilities could be traced to specific codes in the chart of accounts.

This information was not produced with the needs of businesses in mind. It was not readily available, nor of much assistance in the day-to-day operations or as an aid to reaching business decisions. The accounting framework was to a large extent cash based. There were little or no provisions for bad debts or obsolete stock. Depreciation was recorded at fixed rates which were usually lower than those adopted in the West. Company accountants were primarily bookkeepers, their prime responsibility being to ensure that accounts complied with the appropriate laws and regulations. These rules effectively removed any subjective element from accounting practices: accountants were not involved in the decision making nor in monitoring profitability and budgets.

Participants in the market economy, both domestic and foreign investors, need information about the financial position of companies in which they are to invest. Not only are there differences between Hungarian and other accounting systems themselves. In 1991, IBUSZ reported a net profit of Ft404 million based on Hungarian accounting standards, but when these were restated, the results showed profits of only Ft6.4 million. Investors looking at the performance of a company over time would face difficulties weighing factors which previously affected the performance of the company such as subsidies, production targets and fixed prices, barter trade and trade conducted in 'transferable' roubles, employment and social benefits policies. Many Hungarian companies have a significant amount of unnecessary assets, which will have to be written down. Appropriate value for land is difficult to determine: outside Budapest, very little land has changed hands. Environmental clean up costs and the identification of environmental risks remain to be determined.

The Act on Accounting

The Act on Accounting came into effect on 1 January 1992. Its purpose is to introduce accounting regulations which are in line with international accounting principles, such as going concern, consistency, prudence and matching. The aim is to ensure the production of information which is sufficiently comprehensive and accurate to enable a true and fair view to be obtained on the income and financial position of a company.

A new relationship is developing between accounting and tax regulations. They are now to operate independently of each other. The taxable income and the amount of tax to be paid are determined under the Corporations Tax Act, but accounting income is defined by the Act on Accounting. The Act outlines the bookkeeping requirements, defines the basic principles to be followed in the preparation of the financial reports, and sets out what needs to be disclosed and published. There is now an element of choice in the methods of valuing assets and liabilities: companies will be able to select the appropriate principles on which to base their accounting systems. The Act, which establishes the role of the independent auditor, applies to all business organisations with the exception of foreign entrepreneurs who have a majority holding in a business operating, but not registered, in Hungary.

The importance of the changes cannot be overemphasised. Accountants are being transformed from bookkeepers to managers of financial information and are being encouraged to take more responsibility for the information they process. Retraining and the developments of the profession are being supervised by the Ministry of Finance.

Books of accounts

The Act on Accounting contains detailed regulations concerning organisations of various types and sizes. Books of account must be kept in forints and must follow Hungarian accounting practices. Only companies operating in a customs-free zone may keep their books in foreign currency. Under the Act the application of a uniform chart of accounts is no longer mandatory. However, companies must establish a chart of accounts based on the uniform chart prescribed in the Act, but which takes into consideration its own goals and conditions. The main goal of the chart is to facilitate the organisation of bookkeeping and financial reporting.

Reporting

Most companies incorporated in the Trade Register and keeping double or single entry books will be required to file their annual accounts. The accounting year is the calendar year. The requirements to publish financial statements are to gradually become more stringent (see Table 13.1).

Table 13.1 *Publishing accounts – the timetable*

Sales revenue	Date of entry into force
In excess of Ft1 billion	1 January 1994
In excess of Ft300 million	1 January 1996
All organisations required to use double entry bookkeeping	1 January 1998

The annual report is intended to show a true picture of the net assets, financial and income position of a company, and contains:

- a balance sheet;

- an income statement;

- notes to the accounts (the 'Supplement'); and

- a business report.

Comparative figures are required, and accounting policies adopted, the names of the principal shareholders, details of liabilities due in five years or more and other financial obligations, movements on tangible and intangible assets and the average number of employees must be disclosed in the notes to the accounts. The business report evaluates the data contained in the accounts and supports the picture drawn from the accounts. As of 1 January 1995, all companies with a majority or decisive control in another company will have to prepare a consolidated annual report.

The annual report must be filed with the Court of Registration by 31 May following the balance sheet date. The business report need not be filed. Companies limited by shares, limited companies with a prime capital in excess of Ft50 million and single person limited companies must publish their accounts together with the auditor's report (but not the business report). Small companies may prepare a simplified annual report which consists of a balance sheet and an income statement with notes to the accounts.

Auditing

Recent economic changes required a new approach to auditing. Under the previous economic system, auditing was limited to checking compliance with economic regulations. Now, the independent auditor's function is not only to check if the company's books and records comply with legislative provisions, but also to examine them in order to determine whether they provide a true and fair view of its net assets at the balance sheet date and reflect accurately its profits and financial position in accordance with generally accepted accounting standards.

Companies limited by shares, limited liability companies with a stock capital of more than Ft50 million and single person companies must appoint independent auditors before the balance sheet date. By 1 January 1998, all entities that maintain double entry bookkeeping will be required to have their financial statements audited. In the case of the transformation of state-owned companies into business associations, the transforming balance sheet also should be independently audited in accordance with the Law on Transformation. If a company limited by shares is to trade its shares publicly, the financial statements contained in the prospectus must also be independently audited in accordance with the Law on Securities and the Stock Exchange.

VALUATION OF ASSETS

The principle of going concern should be assumed when valuing balance sheet items. Principles of consistency should also be applied. Policies applied in previous years should be applied in the next, and all changes in valuation methods and their effect on assets must be explained in the notes to the accounts. The notes to the accounts should contain the valuation procedures applied, the method of depreciation used and the information necessary to provide a realistic picture of the business.

Assets and liabilities

Assets are valued at purchase or production cost. Assets are not to be valued at higher than their historical cost. Tangible and intangible assets (with the exception of land, forests and objects of art) are depreciated over their expected useful lives. Liabilities are valued in the balance sheet at their book value, taking into account foreign currency translation rules if appropriate.

Fixed assets

Fixed assets are to be recorded at cost. They are to be depreciated over their expected useful life. Where the value of the fixed asset has permanently reduced at the date of preparation of the balance sheet then additional depreciation should be charged to reflect market value.

Debtors

The concept of prudence calls for the anticipation of losses when these are certain to be realised. A high level of bad debt in the balance sheet of Hungarian enterprises has been usual. During 1989–1991 debtors in the balance sheet frequently represented more than one-third of gross assets. The amount included cumulative debts which had not been written off over the years. Now specific reserves may be deducted from receivables overdue and bad debts. The provision amounts must be detailed in the notes to the accounts in accordance with the legislation.

Foreign currency transactions

Foreign currency transactions remain restricted because the Hungarian forint is not fully convertible. Monetary assets and liabilities are generally translated at the official rate of exchange. Income and expenses denominated in foreign cur-

rency are translated at the exchange rate published by the
National Bank on the date of the transaction.

Leases

There is no mention of accounting for leases in the legislation,
and there is no distinction between operating and finance leases.

Investment

Long-term investments are recorded at cost with provision for
valuation at market value under certain circumstances.

Goodwill

Goodwill is to be written off over a period of not less than 5 years
but not more than 15 years. If the period is greater than 5 years,
this is to be disclosed in the accounts.

Stocks

Stocks may be valued at acquisition cost, using FIFO (first in
first out), LIFO (last in first out) or weighted average. The FIFO
method is strongly recommended by the Ministry of Finance. At
the end of the accounting year, the lower of cost or market value
is used for inventory valuation. Provisions for obsolete stock are
to be set aside in specific reserves.

Valuation and privatisation

An important element in the privatisation process and indeed in
any change of ownership is the adoption of clear and rigorous
valuation policies in order to determine the value to be put on the
business from the point of view of both the seller and the buyer.
One of the problems which have undermined progress in
privatising companies is the difficulty in valuing enterprises and
determining reasonable prices. If prices are set too high, this will
discourage foreign investors. If they are perceived to be too low,
sensitivities will be aroused.

The State Property Agency (SPA) needs to determine fair
value to support its negotiations with investors and to justify the
sales price of a company to its political masters (and the
population at large). The decision to reverse the sale of a 50 per
cent stake in the hotel chain HungarHotel, to a Swedish
company, was made following popular outcry on the grounds
that the foreign investor was getting the assets on the cheap.
One popular misconception is that the book value represents the
market value. Companies make unrealistic assumptions, based

on historical trends, about future costs and assume the continued availability of cheap raw materials and energy and low labour costs (often offset by low productivity) and revenues, for example where demand may have literally exploded following the collapse of communism but now has levelled off.

Investors (and lenders) are concerned with the earnings potential of the proposed investment in the light of the risks involved and the contribution they will have to make in order to achieve the desired level of profitability. A foreign investor will look at the profit record, accounting policies, cash flow, the prospects of the company, its products, its management, the breadth and depth of their experience, the costs involved in restructuring, the risks of a non-convertible currency, a changing economy and increased competition from imports.

The Ministry of Finance has set out the regulations governing the valuation of companies to be privatised. For trade sales, which involves a competitive bidding process, an independent market valuation has to be submitted. It should be borne in mind that the methods of valuation used in the privatisation process are undergoing continuous evolution.

14

The Fiscal Framework

KPMG Peat Marwick

The Hungarian tax system has undergone a process of gradual reform over the past five years to meet the challenges of a free market. The most radical measures were introduced in 1988 when both a value added tax (VAT) and a personal income tax were introduced. At the same time the system of company taxation was streamlined. The system of turnover tax, with more than 100 different rates, was dropped. At the same time the Economic Associations Act was introduced. The basic framework is still undergoing changes to adapt to the changing economic conditions and to meet Western standards.

TAX ADMINISTRATION

The Tax and Financial Auditing Office is the principle taxing authority. As the name suggests, a major part of their role is the supervision of the accuracy of the returns.

A major challenge is to translate legal reforms into administrative action. The number of taxpaying units has increased dramatically, but this has been accompanied by a reduced level of compliance. This is true not only for private entrepreneurs, conducting their business on a cash basis, but also for state enterprises that have gained managerial autonomy. The Hungarian Ministry of Finance is moving on several fronts in order to reduce the ballooning budget deficit. New regulations have been laid to capture for the tax authorities a larger share of the estimated Ft5 billion in undeclared income. Companies will be struck from the commercial registry if they do not satisfy the tax collectors within 30 days that their tax affairs are in order.

CORPORATE INCOME TAX

The Corporations Tax Act (CTA) was introduced in January 1992 to bring company taxation into line with the new Accountancy Act, which was simultaneously introduced. In accordance with the principle of neutrality of competition, the same system is applicable to all state companies, co-operatives, economic associations (including joint ventures) and private entrepreneurs. Companies with their head office in Hungary are treated as resident and are liable to tax on their world-wide income. Non-resident companies only pay tax if they have a permanent establishment, or derive income from a source in Hungary (subject to the provisions of the double taxation treaties entered into by Hungary).

The basis of assessment is the profit shown in the financial statements and adjusted according to the CTA. The standard rate of taxation drops from 40 per cent to 36 per cent in 1994. Capital gains are included in taxable income and are taxed at the standard rate. Companies are allowed to carry forward losses for five years. In addition, companies established after 1 January 1992 and without a predecessor, may carry forward their start-up losses for the first three years. Companies are allowed to make provisions against specific amounts of non-performing loans. Capital assets may be depreciated for tax purposes according to the depreciation schedules found in the CTA.

Anti-avoidance

The CTA has introduced arm's length principles in respect of transactions between related parties. The tax authorities may substitute a fair market value if payments of service fees, royalties, etc are not effected at arm's length prices.

A thin capitalisation rule came into force on 1 January 1993. The amount of interest on loans granted by companies owning more than 25 per cent of the share capital of the borrower is disallowed on the excess for tax purposes if the amount of the loan exceeds four times the capital of the borrower.

Incentives

Joint ventures are entitled to the same tax allowances that are granted to Hungarian companies. Until December 1993, there were a number of tax breaks available to companies with a qualifying foreign participation (30 per cent and a total capital of at least Ft50 million). The deadline has been extended for companies which had commenced 'particularly important' business prior to the end of 1993. These companies will need to show that they have commenced construction or purchased at least a single piece of equipment before they can enjoy the following tax incentives:

- a 60 per cent reduction in the rate of taxation for 5 years where more than half of income derives from the manufacture of goods, followed by a reduction of 40 per cent for the next 5 years

- a 100 per cent tax reduction for 5 years if more than half the income originates from specified activities which include telecommunications, biotechnology and agriculture, followed by a 60% reduction for the next 5 years.

The government proposes more selective tax credits for dividend reinvestment as well as tax reductions for investment in environmentally friendly production and for investments which create employment in Hungary. For the first time, tax breaks will be available to Hungarian investors as well as foreign investors. An alternative has been proposed for companies which yield substantial revenues from the production of environmental products or high technology. The government may on application provide a 10 year tax incentive to companies with a maximum 100 per cent credit for 5 years and 60 per cent for the next 5 years.

Minimum tax

In order to extract tax from loss-making companies which are not paying corporation tax, a new so-called minimum tax will operate from 1994. The minimum tax is computed as 2 per cent of a corporation's adjusted revenues.

Assessment and collection

Corporation tax is payable on a self-assessment system. The company must determine the amount of tax to be paid, file its preliminary annual return by 28 February for the previous tax year and pay its tax. The final return is due by 31 May of the following year. Resident companies make advance payment of tax twice a month, while foreign companies make advance payments every quarter.

Taxation of foreign companies

The Corporate Income Tax Act distinguishes between foreign companies which carry on business activities in Hungary through a permanent establishment and those that do not. The definition of a permanent establishment is wide and includes offices, branches, construction sites, places of management and places where services are provided by a foreign company. However, in practice permanent establishments may only be set up in the form of a representative office.

If a permanent establishment exists, the foreign company must pay a form of branch tax. The tax base is the difference between revenue and expenses, and under no circumstances can the base be less than 10 per cent of revenue. A 10 per cent deduction is allowed to cover head office expenses. The company must comply with the tax rules applicable to resident companies.

A foreign company which obtains income, such as royalty fees, payments for know-how, copyright, interest and artistic fees, without having a site in Hungary is liable to corporation tax, but the tax is reduced by 50 per cent. The payer withholds the tax and remits it to the Hungarian authorities. There is no withholding tax on dividends paid to corporate shareholders. The provisions of the double taxation treaties signed by Hungary, which override domestic tax legislation, may limit the tax liability of foreign companies by restricting the scope of what constitutes a permanent establishment or reducing the rates of withholding taxes payable.

PERSONAL TAXES

Income tax is payable on all types of income, which must be aggregated to calculate the tax base. The highest marginal tax rate is 44 per cent as of 1 January 1994. Also from 1994, all interest receipts are subject to a withholding of 10 per cent.

Employers withhold an advance payment of personal income tax from salaries and wages. Employees have to pay the difference between the final sum payable and the total sum of the advance payments made to the tax authorities by the annual deadline (generally mid-March).

Expatriates

Expatriates working in Hungary must pay tax under the same rules that apply for Hungarians. If they spend more than 183 days in Hungary, they are treated as residents and pay tax on their worldwide income. There is, however, a special concession. Only 70 per cent of their remuneration will be subject to tax provided that he or she is employed by a foreign company or one which is partly or wholly foreign owned.

The payment of housing or the provision of a car are subject to taxation.

Non-residents

Foreigners are subject to income tax on the income they receive from sources within Hungary. This includes employment income, business activities and gains.

SOCIAL SECURITY AND PAYROLL LEVIES

Three levies on payroll in the form of social security, unemployment (solidarity fund) and education fund contributions represent the main source of finance for the social security system and unemployment benefit. These levies have risen sharply in recent years and represent a significant cost of doing business in Hungary, as employers must pay 52.7 per cent of gross salaries irrespective of the profitability of the enterprise. The current rate of social security is 44 per cent and 7.2 per cent goes to the unemployment fund. The rates for employees are 10 per cent and 2 per cent of their gross wages, respectively. In addition, employers pay 1.5 per cent to the education fund. Companies with foreign participation are exempt from social security contributions for their non-Hungarian employees, but not from the contribution to the unemployment fund.

LOCAL TAXES

Municipalities must increasingly rely on their own resources to pay for the cost of providing services because the central government has reduced its contribution to their finances. Local governments have permission to levy a property tax, a community tax, a tourism tax and a commercial/business tax. Rates and the types of tax levied vary from locality to locality. The business tax may use turnover or number of employees as a criterion. Investors should understand their potential liabilities before establishing or expanding operations in a specific locality. The business tax could be as high as 0.8 per cent of turnover in 1993. The tax is also payable by foreign companies with permanent establishments in Hungary.

Conversely, localities may wish to attract foreign investors. For example in Győr, a foreign investor building a facility in the newly created industrial park will not have to pay the local business tax.

VAT AND EXCISE

VAT (called AFA in Hungary) legislation has been completely overhauled and, as of 1993, is in line with the EC's Sixth Directive. It is a consumption tax, borne in full by the final consumer of the product or service. There are three rates of VAT:

- a standard 25 per cent rate;

- a reduced rate of 10 per cent which applies to most foodstuffs, books and medical equipment, equipment for environmental protection; and

- a zero rate for medicine.

VAT is levied where services or goods are supplied in Hungary and on the import of goods and services. Individuals engaged in business activities are liable to VAT. Liability to tax arises at the time of performance which is generally the one stated in the contract. However, a foreign investor's 'in kind' contribution which is imported from abroad free of import duties, is subject to VAT.

In cases of reciprocity, foreign companies which are registered for VAT abroad may claim reimbursement of VAT paid in Hungary by means of a special refund procedure. Services supplied by foreign enterprises might attract VAT depending on where the activity is deemed to be performed. The liability may either arise for the company rendering the service if it is considered a domestic taxpayer or for the recipient of the services.

The tax base includes intangibles, goodwill and membership fees. The export of goods is not subject to VAT. The availability of tax-free treatment of the export of services depends on where the service is deemed to have been performed.

Excise taxes

The most significant excise taxes apply to petrol, tobacco and other luxury items. Importers must pay the tax on import. The taxable base is the declared customs value.

15

Property

SJ Berwin & Co

A knowledge of the basic legal rules relating to the acquisition and disposal of property (here meaning land and buildings as opposed to personal property) and rights encumbering land is important to the potential investor because the land occupied by an enterprise may be of paramount importance. The law, however, is currently in a state of flux. There is a proposal to introduce a comprehensive new property law in parliament, which will bring the ownership, use and disposal of land in line with the current trend towards a market economy. The following explanation of current property law is based upon provisions of the Civil Code, the Land Act (Act I of 1987) and decrees made pursuant to that Act, although both will be radically amended or repealed by the new property law. There is also a brief consideration of the Compensation Act (Act XXV of 1991) at the conclusion of this chapter.

It should be said at the outset that many of the property provisions in the Civil Code date from the time of the socialist republic. Many of these principles are no longer followed and indeed are inappropriate in the emerging market economy. However, the principles of property law which are based on the concepts contained in the Austrian/German Civil Codes will survive the transition to a market economy, although of course it is likely that they will be expanded.

The holding of property in Hungary is generally based upon the concept of ownership prevalent in the Austrian/German Civil Code, rather than the English forms of tenure and estates. Act I of 1987 deals with the concepts and basic principles of state and private ownership of land, its acquisition and disposal, and contain some particular provisions for regulating and protecting agricultural land. The Act also contains a general concept that land is a national treasure and that the protection of land, its proper use and its disposal must be in the interests of society as a whole.

OWNERSHIP

Land may be owned by the state or any other legal entity, including private individuals. The owner of land acquires ownership of everything that subsequently becomes part of the land, except produce due to a third party.

The owner of land is entitled to use it and collect profits from it but is subject to any matters which burden it. The owner's possession is protected and he may assign the benefit of the profits in the land or transfer title to it.

The Civil Code defines the occasions when ownership of property may be acquired in Hungary. These provisions apply equally to Hungarian and foreign individuals and organisations wishing to purchase property. In addition to the contract or other means of transfer of ownership, the change in ownership must be registered in the Land Register (Decree 31 of 1972 on the Registration of Real Property). The usual means of acquiring property are as follows:

- by contract of sale and purchase (see below);
- by exchange of property;
- by gift;
- by prescription (where someone has possessed the property, other than through criminal action, violence, or objectionable behaviour, as his own for 10 years without interruption);
- contract of maintenance or life annuity contract; and
- inheritance and court order.

The state is a legal person in the same way as individuals and therefore it may own property in exactly the same way. Property is actually managed on behalf of the state by the founding body of the user/occupier (ie, the ministry or State Property Agency) and where the land is not administered by a state organisation it is managed by the local authority. The manager exercises all the rights of the owner (he may lease the land but may not mortgage it) and can transfer the right to manage the property to another state manager where this is considered appropriate.

A purchaser of property in state ownership should be aware of the provisions on the protection of state property contained in the Sale Utilisation and Protection of Assets Temporarily Owned by the State Act (Act LIV of 1992). If the value of the property exceeds Ft20 million the state enterprise must report the proposed sale to the State Property Agency (SPA), irrespective of how the property is to be disposed of (ie, sale/purchase, exchange or lease). If the state enterprise sells other property, all sales over a two-year period are aggregated and the same limit, with the same consequences, applies to the aggregate value. This rule does not apply where the state enterprise is selling the property as its regular business.

Where a state enterprise makes an 'in kind' contribution to a business association the contract must be reported to SPA if the contribution exceeds 10 per cent of the enterprise's asset value or if the value of the contribution is more than Ft20 million.

Finally, all contracts must be reported (including leases) where more than 50 per cent of a state enterprise's assets are utilised by a third party who also enjoys the profits.

A state enterprise may not dispose of the property in any of the above cases prior to reporting to SPA. Following such reporting, SPA may order a revaluation, oblige the enterprise to seek competitive tender, impose conditions on the sale or refuse approval where the contract violates the interests of Hungarian society or causes damage to the national economy. If none of these measures are taken within 30 days the contract may be concluded.

In relation to property owned by a local authority, permission of the Committee Supervising Property is required.

ACQUISITION OF PROPERTY BY FOREIGNERS

The Land Act (Act 1 of 1987) provides for those cases where foreign private individuals and legal entities require permission to purchase property. For the purposes of the Act, foreign private individuals are non-Hungarian citizens and Hungarian citizens whose permanent place of residence is abroad. Unless another law or international treaty provides otherwise, foreign private individuals or legal entities may only acquire property in Hungary with the permission of the Ministry of Finance. The Ministry of Finance grants permission in conjunction with other competent/interested ministers. This requirement applies to sale/purchase, gift or exchange, but not to other methods of acquisition such as inheritance or prescription. Permission of the Ministry of Finance is also required to take a lease.

However, a 1991 amendment to the Land Act allows a foreign person to acquire property with the permission of the Ministry of Finance provided:

- it does not violate the interests of the Hungarian state, local authorities or tourist, cultural, social welfare or other social interests; or

- the foreigner's property in Hungary had been expropriated; or

- the foreigner exchanged certain real estate in Hungary for other real estate in Hungary; or

- the reason for acquisition is to eliminate joint ownership.

The Foreign Investment Act (Act XXIV of 1988) enables business associations with foreign participation registered in Hungary to purchase property necessary for their economic activities as contained in the articles of association (or founders' deed) without the need for any permission. The business association may freely dispose of property by sale, lease or mortgage. The same provisions apply to the acquisition of leases.

DISTINCTION BETWEEN LAND AND BUILDINGS

Generally, ownership of a building lies with the owner of the land. However, the Civil Code draws a distinction between land and the building erected upon it in certain circumstances. Ownership resides with the builder where this is provided for by an Act or an agreement concluded in writing with the owner of land. There is a mutual option for the owner of the land over the building and the owner of the building over the land. If the ownership of a building is acquired by the builder, the owner of the building has a right to use the land while the building remains in the land.

RIGHTS AND DUTIES OF LANDOWNERS

The Civil Code lays down various rights and duties on an owner of land. However, as many of these stem from the time of the socialist republic, they are directed (although not specifically so) more to the individual householder than the business owner. However, until repealed they reflect the only existing principles of law. The main principles are as follows:

- an owner has a right of possession and is entitled to protection of that possession;

- an owner may not deprive adjoining buildings of support;

- an owner must permit entry on to his land for the purpose of carrying out public works, in return for compensation;

- an owner may use neighbouring land in order to carry out demolition, construction or repair work on his land, in return for compensation;

- boundaries separating different parcels of land are party boundaries and the costs of maintenance are borne in accordance with the size of the parcels;

- an owner must permit state organisations authorised by statute (mainly utilities but also mining co-operatives) to temporarily use the property for the purposes of their activities, subject to being indemnified against damage;

- several persons may have property rights on different portions of the property; and

- each co-owner is entitled to possess and use the property and neither co-owner shall exercise their rights so as to ignore the rights and legal interest of the others.

DEALINGS WITH LAND

The Civil Code gives a right to the owner of land to give up possession of the land itself, or the profits from that land (the so-called usufruct prevalent in civil law countries but not in England), to give it as security, to encumber it and to transfer ownership. Land in Hungary is subject to a system of registration which is thought to be fairly reliable and accurate. Where ownership of the land and building is with one person, the ownership of the land and building must be transferred together (although this rule does not apply to the state which may separate the two).

Any disposal in breach of a statutory provision will be null and void. The right to dispose of or encumber land may be excluded or restricted only by the terms of the contract at the time of disposal, but only so as to protect the rights of the transferor. Such a restriction must be entered on the Land Register. A disposal of land contrary to such restriction is null and void, provided the restriction has been noted on the Land Register and unless the purchaser has purchased otherwise than in good faith and not for value.

The usual method for the disposal of land is by a contract for the sale of land. The principles applicable to the formation of contracts generally, and specifically contracts of sale, are explained in Chapter 16, and are equally applicable to contracts for the sale of land. Generally the parties are free to agree on the terms of the contract. The important requirements for a contract for the sale and transfer of land are that:

- it must be in writing;

- it must be clear as to the seller and the buyer and as to the exact extent of the land to be sold;

- the price and the conditions of payment must be defined;

- the seller is under an obligation to disclose encumbrances;

- unless otherwise provided in the contract the vendor bears the cost of proving title to the land in the Land Register;

- unless otherwise provided in the contract the purchaser bears the cost of concluding the contract, preparing the transfer and effecting change of ownership in the Land Register.

Although the contract and transfer theoretically may be contained in separate documents, contemporary practice generally relies on one document.

A duty is payable by the purchaser (unless it is agreed that the vendor pays it) and this is currently equal to 2 per cent of the market value in the case of a flat, or otherwise 5 per cent of the market value. There is a Land Registry fee (currently Ft2000) payable by the purchaser, unless the vendor has agreed to pay it.

The parties may agree that possession and transfer of ownership occur at different times. A purchaser may sign the contract and simultaneously enter into possession of the property, but the seller retains ownership until the price is paid.

A right of pre-emption (first refusal) may be incorporated in the contract. The seller may also require a right to repurchase the property over a maximum period of five years. The repurchase price will be the original price plus the increase in value due to improvements carried out by the original purchaser less the reduction in value due to use. An option to purchase is similar to a right to buy back, but it can be granted to a person other than the former owner. The maximum period for the option is six months.

It is usual to pay a deposit upon the signing of the contract. A distinction must be drawn between a deposit and an advance payment. If the contract is fulfilled the deposit is included within the purchase price. If the contract is not fulfilled as a result of a mistake of the purchaser, the deposit is lost. If the seller is at fault he pays back twice the amount of the deposit. If neither or both is responsible for non-fulfilment, the deposit is returned.

Within 30 days of the conclusion of the contract of sale and purchase the contract must be submitted to the Land Registry. Any approval required for the validating of the contract (eg approval of the Ministry of Finance for a foreign purchaser, or the waiver of a right of pre-emption) must also be submitted. The transfer of ownership is legally effected once registration is completed and the ownership is retrospective to the date of transfer.

Decree 31 of 1972 on the registration of real property contains detailed provisions regulating the registration of interests in, and ownership of land, similar to the system of land registration in Germany. In addition, the provisions of the Civil Code enable a person to become an owner of land by auction provided the vendor possesses good title.

The Civil Code also states specifically that ownership of land can be acquired by prescription – that is, adverse possession for a continuous period of 10 years. However, ownership of part of the land cannot be acquired by prescription where it has been acquired unlawfully or where it is indivisible from the whole. An adverse possessor who does not have his ownership entered in the Land Register cannot claim against any third party purchaser for value.

LEASES AND RIGHTS OF USE

A foreign firm may wish to acquire accommodation without acquiring ownership. Two alternatives are lease and right to use.

Leases

The concept of a lease differs in the Hungarian civil law system from the English common law system. In Hungary a lease does not take effect as an interest in land but as a mere contract of tenancy giving a right to occupy the premises upon the terms and conditions agreed between the landlord and tenant. The Civil Code contains a basic framework of the law. These provisions are largely dispositive rather than mandatory, which means that they may be excluded by agreement. The provisions are largely ignored by the parties to the lease because they are relevant to the occupation of apartments during the period of the socialist republic rather than to commercial lettings. Landlords and tenants prefer instead to be bound by the terms of their own agreements, although of course, where the lease does not exclude the provisions of the Civil Code, these will apply. Therefore, a brief mention of the Civil Code provisions is required.

The lease must be concluded in writing. The landlord and tenant are free to agree the term (either a definite or indefinite period) and the rent, subject to any rental controls in existence at the time (rent controls exist for apartments owned by the state but not for commercial premises). There is a provision enabling possession by the tenant prior to agreement on the rent with subsequent agreement for determination by the court. This provision is unlikely to be applied in commercial transactions, but this may of course be relevant to lease renewals where the old rent will be payable until the new rent has been agreed.

Responsibility for repairs and permitted alterations are again a matter for agreement, and similarly any service charge that may be payable to the landlord. Tenants are entitled to claim a reduction in their rent during the time that the landlord does not repair the premises in accordance with his contractual obligations or if the landlord prevents the use of the premises. The amount of reduction is agreed or otherwise fixed by the court. Furthermore, the tenant may obtain reimbursement of any expenses incurred in repairing the premises where the landlord is in default. Smaller expenses incurred in the maintenance of the premises are borne by the tenant, and other expenses as well as rates and taxes are borne by the landlord.

The landlord may terminate the lease if the tenant fails to pay the rent, damages the property, improperly uses the premises or prevents the carrying out of repairs or refurbishment works to the building. The tenant may determine a fixed-term lease by giving at least 15 days notice.

The Civil Code is silent about use and assignment. Such matters are obviously for agreement, although in general terms the Civil Code does allow assignment of the benefit of a contract provided notice of the assignment is given. Sub-letting will be governed by the terms of the lease.

As can be seen from this brief explanation, the archaic provisions of the Civil Code are really now not applicable to the commercial letting market. As such therefore, parties will reach their own terms, probably excluding the specific Civil Code provisions and relying upon the general principles of contract law. As yet, there appears to be no local 'market' for the type or style of lease, with foreign investors (and indeed local landlords where such a document has been supplied to them) using forms of lease compatible to their jurisdiction with the rent payable in convertible currency.

Right to use

Premises in state or local authority ownership may be the subject of the grant of a right to use the premises. A public competition is held for empty premises and the person submitting the highest fee is generally successful. If a successful bidder withdraws he must pay the expenses of the competition. The right to use is generally for an indefinite period unless the bidder only requires the premises, or the premises are only available, for a temporary period.

As mentioned previously, the civil law possesses a property law concept of usufruct which is the right of a person to take the 'fruits' or profits of the land owned by another. This concept is also contained in Hungarian property law and the main principles are:

- the usufruct is enforeable against successors in title and remains in force until the death of the beneficiary unless a shorter period is agreed;

- the right generally must be entered on the Land Register to be effective;

- the right is capable of assignment;

- the beneficiary of the usufruct is responsible for maintenance of the property but may not carry out alterations to the property;

- the owner must be notified of any impending danger to the property; and

- the property must be delivered back upon determination of the usufruct, and the beneficiary of the usufruct is obliged to pay damages in relation to damage caused to the property.

Although still of conceptual importance the usufruct is of little practical significance in commercial transactions (other than of course to beware of it when acquiring property), being restricted principally to family settlements.

MORTGAGES

Although the provisions of the Civil Code (as explained in this section) recognise the possibility of mortgage, the principles are very bare, evidencing the lack of a sophisticated property investment market. The main principles in the Civil Code are:

- a mortgage contract which entitles a mortgagee to possess, use or collect proceeds from the mortgaged property, is null and void;

- a mortgage may only be entered into to secure a money claim and must be in excess of Ft5000;

- the mortgage contract must be in writing and must be registered in the Land Register to become effective;

- the amount of indebtedness must also be noted, and where the indebtedness is an open facility the upper limit of the facility must be noted;

- further advances may be tacked on to the original mortgage;

- the mortgage may be secured upon the whole of the mortgagor's immovable property or only part of it;

- the mortgagee may take action to prevent the owner endangering its security; and

- in the case of a breach of the mortgage contract, the mortgagor may satisfy the debt from the mortgaged property.

EASEMENTS/SERVITUDES

The owner of property may obtain rights (an easement/ servitude) across another person's property. These may be obtained for the purpose of access, supply of drainage and water, support to a building or a similar purpose. An owner of land may also obtain a right of way across a neighbour's land for the purpose of access to a highway where no other access is available.

The main principles covering such rights are:

- the existence of the rights must be entered on the Land Register of the land affected by them;

- the right may be obtained by prescription after it has been exercised continuously for ten years;

- the right attaches to the land and may not be sold separately;

- in exercising the right, the rights of the affected landowner must be respected;

- where the right is used in common with other persons, maintenance is borne in proportion to use; and

- the right ceases if it is not exercised for a period of 10 years.

PROTECTION OF RIGHTS OF OWNERSHIP

All owners are guaranteed the right to possession of their property. Where another is deprived of possession by a person with no legal title, or is prevented from enjoying his property by way of unlawful interference, the owner is entitled to protection by way of an action similar to that for trespass in England.

The owner must apply to the special administrative organ (a local authority body) which is under a duty to restore the land to the owner and to restrain the trespasser from continuing his conduct. The special administrative organ also has discretion to award damages and costs to the owner. The decision of the special administrative organ must be made within 3 days of application. The aggrieved party has 15 days in which to appeal.

RESTITUTION/COMPENSATION

The Compensation Act (Act XXV of 1991) was passed to compensate former owners of land unlawfully expropriated (ie obtained for a price less than the market value) and brief details of the Act are as follows:

- The law will only apply to expropriation after 8 June 1949 (although limited compensation is due for expropriations under certain stated enactments passed between 1 May 1939 and 8 June 1949).

- The current economic situation in Hungary does not allow for there to be compensation at full market value, and compensation other than for farm land will be assessed on the basis of an amount of forints per square metre or, in the case of a business, an amount of forints per number of employees on an ascending scale.

- There will be no restitution of land to former owners. However, in relation to agricultural land only, the original land or land of equivalent value may be given to the former owners. Otherwise, compensation will be based upon income from land expressed in gold crowns and converted into forints.

- The form of compensation will be in vouchers, with a value calculated as a descending percentage of the actual compensation payable up to a maximum of Ft5 million.

- The voucher holder will be able to use the vouchers to purchase state assets, but the voucher is not redeemable by the state.

- During the period that the voucher is not used it will attract interest. The voucher may be freely sold by the holder.

- A proportion of the assets in the privatisation programme will be set aside for voucher holders, amounting to Ft100 million out of the total programme of Ft1800 million.

16

Commercial Law

SJ Berwin & Co

A knowledge of the basic principles of Hungarian commercial law is important for business people because these principles will underlie their business activities in Hungary. This chapter is concerned with the legal framework within which business people will have to work when entering into contracts in Hungary (including a specific type of contract – the sales contract) and covering certain aspects of business activities including liability for damage to others, unjust enrichment and competition law. With the need for improved infrastructure, there is also a brief consideration of the Concessions Act (Act XVI of 1991). Other practical aspects of commercial law including intellectual property, distributorship agreements, franchises and agency are dealt with in other chapters.

Hungary does not possess a distinct commercial code containing provisions relevant only to commercial relations, and the basic principles of commercial law are to be found in the Civil Code.

LAW

From a practical point of view a business contract entered into in Hungary will normally be in writing with the terms agreed between the parties fully documented. The terms will be a matter of commercial agreement and when agreement is reached the contract will be executed and the parties bound to perform their respective obligations. In Hungary (as indeed generally in all other systems of law) there are some very basic principles that govern the formation, interpretation and termination of contracts.

What is a contract and when is it made? The answer is generally found in the Hungarian Civil Code, the provisions of which relating to contracts are very similar to those contained in the Austrian and German Civil Code.

Persons legally able to contract

Who can enter into contracts? All Hungarian individuals except legally incapable people (including minors under 14 years and persons with mental incapacity) have the capacity to contract. The same legal personality has been extended to entities such as enterprises, foreign trade organisations and state-owned and private companies. Recognised legal entities include the state, state enterprises, social and business organisations and trade unions. A contract may also be concluded by a representative/agent on behalf of a principal. As under English contract law, there are various provisions in the Civil Code protecting third parties who contract with an agent in good faith, and remedies for the principal against the agent if the agent exceeds his authority.

Meaning of contract

What is a contract and when is it made? A contract is defined by the Civil Code as 'an obligation to perform services and an entitlement to claim services'. Although 'services' is the word used in the translation of the Civil Code, a contract is obviously more general in nature, being a binding mutual obligation; it no doubt also includes goods. A unilateral decision by one party to perform certain acts or deliver goods or services will not generally be binding; only in very few cases determined by statute (for example a donation) will such an undertaking be binding on the person making it. As with English contract law there must normally be two parties making a mutual decision to contract; the contract is formed upon the acceptance by one party of an offer by another.

Freedom to contract

Hungarian law recognises the doctrine of party autonomy, allowing the parties freely to negotiate and agree the terms of the contract provided always that the terms agreed are not prohibited by statute. A contract term which is contrary to a mandatory provision of the Civil Code will be null and void, but there are few such provisions in Hungarian law. Generally, the rules in the Civil Code apply only where the parties are silent as to their specific requirements and obligations – hence the preference always to be as specific as possible and agree on the terms rather than allow the Civil Code to be implied.

Hungarian contract law allows parties to enter into a binding commitment to enter into a subsequent contract – ie, a contract to contract. Such a contract is entered into where the parties would like to be legally bound early and where there are terms still to be agreed. If the terms of the later contract cannot be agreed, the court is empowered to make presumptions as to the terms of the contract which would probably have been entered into; of course, if the essential terms were absent from the preliminary contract this is not possible. For this reason one should be careful when reaching agreements in principle to make clear the non-binding nature of the commitment or the 'heads of terms', unless they are intended to be binding.

Generally, contracts can be made either orally or in writing. However, certain contracts are required to be in writing, such as contracts of agency, mortgage, guarantee, sale of land and, significantly, foreign trade contracts. The requirement for the written form means that at least the essential terms of the contract are set down in writing.

The form of contract

Although as mentioned previously, from a practical point of view, contracts will be in writing with fully documented terms, Hungarian contract law contains important theoretical principles that govern the making of a contract. These are:

- an offer to contract is binding on the person making it, unless the person making the offer expressly states otherwise when making it, or stipulates that the offer remains open for a specified period;

- acceptance must be in relation to the original offer, and may be oral or in writing;

- acceptance occurs when it is communicated and comes to the knowledge of the other party and at that time the contract comes into force; and

- if the contract requires the approval of a state authority, the contract does not come into effect until that approval is received.

Restrictions on contract terms

As noted above, the parties are free to decide on the terms of the contract except where there is a mandatory rule to the contrary. The provisions of the civil code are dispositive and will comprise the terms of the contract except where the parties expressly provide otherwise.

Hungarian legislation recognises that a foreign law may govern a contract involving a foreign party, but the choice of such law cannot avoid the application of any Hungarian mandatory legal rules. Generally, Hungarian enterprises will wish contracts with foreign partners to be governed by Hungarian law; an English contracting party will equally prefer English law. The compromise is often for the parties to agree to submit to some neutral jurisdiction, such as German or Swiss law, and this is also acceptable to Hungarian law subject only to mandatory law.

Contract law recognises the need to balance the strength of the contracting parties. Where the bargain from one party is disproportionate to that provided by the other party the contract may be set aside.

Performance of the contract

Contracts are deemed to have been performed by the parties where the obligations have been fulfilled at the stipulated time and place and the goods or services are of the type, quality and quantity contained in the contract. Essentially, where the goods or services have been delivered to the person receiving them and the purchase price paid then the contract is performed.

Void contracts

Where a contract is void, having been induced by fraud, mistake, threats or undue influence or entered into for immoral purposes, it will be treated as never having been concluded. Hungarian law will return the parties to the exact situation they were in before the contract was made. If the original state of affairs cannot be regained, a court may declare the contract valid until the date of its judgement and then make an order as to the future conduct of the parties' relationship or, alternatively, it can remove the offending portion of the agreement and declare the remainder of the contract to be valid. This will naturally depend on the circumstances surrounding the contract and the desirability of perpetuating it.

A person who has acted upon a void contract in good faith may claim compensation from the parties for losses originating from the conclusion of the contract. If any of the parties has acted in bad faith towards a third party they must compensate that third party even if the cause of the contract being void cannot be imputed to their conduct.

Termination of contract

A contract validly concluded may be terminated in various ways:

- breach of contract;
- agreement of the parties; and
- performance being impossible.

Breach of contract

A party to a contract may be responsible to the other for damages sustained by the other as a consequence of the delay or failure in performance of this part of the contract unless he can prove that he used all available means to avoid the delay. Where the delay relates to the payment of money, interest is payable at the statutory rate.

A breach of contract may also arise where one party fails to perform the contract in accordance with its terms. The person suffering from the breach may require the payment of damages or a reduction of the price. Where defective goods are involved, a replacement of the goods may be required unless they are capable of elementary repair. If the repair is not undertaken within a reasonable time then the other party may repair it himself and seek compensation. Defects should be notified immediately as there are limitation periods after expiry of which claims are unenforceable.

Consent

The parties may terminate a contract by consent. If the contract is terminated then future obligations cease and the obligations that have been performed are compensated for.

Impossibility

If performance of the contract becomes impossible due to the fault of neither party the contract will be terminated. A party who becomes aware of an event likely to render performance impossible must inform the other party and is liable for damages if he does not. If the event rendering the performance of the contract impossible is due to the fault of one of the parties then that party may be liable for damages. Where the impossibility of performance is limited to a part only of the contract, this may be severed and the remainder performed.

Exclusion of liability for breach

Liability for wilful or gross negligence and criminal breach of contract and/or a breach of contract causing personal injury or damage to property cannot be excluded by a contractual term. A party may not exclude its liability except where permitted by statute and unless there is also a counterbalancing reduction in price. A contract relating to foreign trade may include exclusion of liability, except the primary liability set out previously.

CONTRACTS FOR SALE

Any form of property (whether movable or immovable) can in principle be the subject of a contract for sale. The following rules therefore apply to all property unless otherwise stated, but it should always be recalled that rights over land must be registered in the Land Register.

The contract itself will be made in accordance with the basic principles contained in the Civil Code. It may be oral or written, unless it is a contract for immovable property (including land), which must be made in writing.

The most noteworthy point about a contract for sale is the duty of disclosure that is imposed on the seller of the goods. The seller must inform the buyer as to the nature of the thing that is to be sold and particularly about any encumbrances that exist over it. Any documentation concerning such encumbrances must be passed to the buyer by the seller.

It is possible for the seller to retain ownership of the property to be sold until the final payment is received, where that is expressly provided by the agreement of the parties. Such a retention of title clause enables the seller to reserve the ability to take repossesion of the property should the buyer default. During this time, the buyer is prevented from disposing of the property. However, where a buyer purchases the property in good faith from the buyer specified by the original contract, before the seller under that contract has been paid the full contractual price, he will be able to claim ownership of the thing to be sold. Importantly, the buyer bears the risk of any damage caused to the property once it has been delivered to him, even though the seller has retained ownership of the property by contract.

Where the third party has rights over the property which prevent the buyer from taking unencumbered ownership of the property and the buyer has no notice of the encumbrances, the buyer can cancel the contract if the seller is unable to remove the rights of that third party. The buyer is entitled to refuse to pay for the goods until the property has been cleared of encumbrances. Alternatively, he can take action to clear the property of encumbrances himself, at the seller's expense, where the seller does not do so within a specified time limit. The seller can exclude any further liability on his part to the extent that he can show he acted in good faith.

Options and first refusal

A person may be given an option to purchase property. The maximum duration of an option is six months. The option may be activated at any time by the buyer communicating his wish to exercise the option to the owner. There is no obligation for its acceptance to be in writing, but obviously to be able to prove acceptance it is better if it is. The owner granting the option will only be relieved of his obligations under it where he satisfies the court that his circumstances have changed to such a degree that forcing him to fulfil his obligation would be unduly onerous. Otherwise the party who granted the option is liable for any damage or loss caused to the thing to be sold.

A person may be given the right of first refusal upon the sale of the property. Where this is the case, the owner must first offer the property to that person at the intended disposal price before the property can be sold. If the person accepts the owner's offer the sale proceeds on the predetermined terms.

Any right to repurchase property must be agreed between the parties at the time of the creation of the contract of sale. The maximum duration for which this right may exist is five years. The repurchase price is the original price increased or decreased by improvements or depreciation.

The parties to a contract can agree that payment for the property will be made in instalments. Where this is the case the seller is allowed to include a term enabling the contract to be terminated where the buyer fails to make any one payment on time, provided that the buyer has been given adequate time to make the payment.

UNJUST ENRICHMENT

Hungarian law has a general principle of unjust enrichment that is wider than anything comparable in English law. Where a person acquires a pecuniary advantage from property to which he does not have title and at the expense of another person, the advantage must be refunded or paid to the person who is properly entitled. Therefore, title to goods may pass to an innocent third party even if the transferor did not have title but the transferor will be responsible to the owner for the purchase price.

LIABILITY FOR ACTIVITIES

Normal activities

A person unlawfully causing damage to another person must compensate that person. He is absolved from such liability if he shows that he was acting in a way that would be generally expected of him in that situation. There is a discretion for the courts to release this liability in whole or part if it is due to special circumstances. This concept follows closely the German concept of delict. Generally, liability for acts causing damage fall upon the perpetrator whether or not he is at fault. An employer may be liable for activities of his employees.

Dangerous operations

A person carrying on a dangerous activity is strictly liable for any damage caused by it unless he can prove that the damage was caused by an outside force over which he had no control.

COMPETITION LAW

The principal law regulating competition is the Competition Act (Act LXXVI of 1990). The supervision of competition is the responsibility of the Office of Economic Competition (OEC).

The Competition Act regulates economic activity within Hungary. Part I of the Act prohibits a number of practices amounting to unfair competition – namely:

- false obligations intended to affect the reputation of a competitor;

- unfairly acquiring, using or disclosing a business secret;

- disrupting or interfering with the establishment of an economic relationship;

- passing off;

- withdrawing or withholding goods or services for the purposes of causing a price increase;

- making delivery or acceptance of goods conditional on delivery and acceptance of other goods; and

- interfering with the fairness of tenders, auctions or stock exchange transactions.

The consumer is also protected against various forms of false, misleading information.

In relation to restriction on competition, the Competition Act largely follows the provisions of the EC Treaty (Articles 85 and 86) that prohibits restrictions on trade and abuses of a dominant economic position. Agreements are unlawful if they restrict or exclude competition. The Act gives examples of the types of cartel which fall within the area of prohibition, including defining the price of goods, dividing the market, excluding a certain group of consumers from the distribution of goods, limiting the choice of the source of the goods and hindering entrance into the market. These rules apply to agreements whether or not they are concluded within Hungary.

There are two exceptions: agreements which are aimed at stopping use of economic power; or agreements of minor significance. An agreement is of minor significance if the total market share of the parties to the agreement does not exceed 10 per cent of the goods sold on the relevant market. The relevant market is defined by taking into account the goods which constitute the subject of the agreement, regional substitutes and geographical area.

The Competition Act permits an exemption to an agreement limiting competition if, first, the limitation is not greater than what is necessary for achieving economically justified common goals and, secondly, the advantages resulting from the agreement exceed the disadvantages. The following are stated to be advantages: favourable tendering prices; improvement in and the maintenance of quality; improvement in the condition of delivery; shortening of the distribution route; rationalisation of the process of purchase and sale; improvement in the selection of goods; fostering of technical and technological development; and improvement of environmental protection or competitiveness in foreign markets. It is a disadvantage if the goods which are the subject of the agreement exceed 30 per cent of the goods sold on the relevant market.

It is unlawful to abuse economic superiority. Economic superiority is presumed when an undertaking's share of the relevant market exceeds 30 per cent. Furthermore, there is deemed to be economic superiority where the share of up to three undertakings exceeds 50 per cent of the open market. The type of conduct which constitutes abuse is extremely wide and the Competition Act only makes mention of some of the most important abuses, including insistence upon unjustified one-sided contractual terms and impediment of access to markets.

Mergers

The questions of market domination and of merger are closely linked. Permission for a merger must be sought from the OEC if:

- the total share of the participants in relation to any goods sold by them exceeds 30 per cent of the relevant market; or

- their joint total revenue from sales in the previous year exceeds Ft10 billion.

The OEC examines the application to determine whether the planned merger hinders the formation, maintenance or development of economic competition. If it does then permission may not be granted. If the OEC concludes that the planned merger would limit competition, then the participants must prove to the OEC either:

- the advantages of the merger exceed the disadvantages; or

- the merger does not exclude economic competition in respect of a majority of the goods in question; or

- the merger promotes transactions on foreign markets that benefit the national economy.

The merger rules also apply where one party obtains decisive influence over another and the parties together have more than 30 per cent of the relevant market. Decisive influence exists where more than 50 per cent of the shares or voting rights in the other have been obtained. Decisive influence may also be deemed even if there is no agreement between the parties to that effect, if it is proved by actual behaviour of the parties.

Parties considering entering into an agreement may apply in advance to the OEC for a determination that the agreement does not unlawfully restrict competition. The application must be made by the parties to the intended merger. The OEC may also initiate proceedings on its own account or at the request of any person who has sustained or may sustain losses resulting from a breach of the Competition Act and where rights or legitimate expectations are affected. There are various time limits for OEC decision making and the majority of its proceedings are held in private. There is no form of appeal other than a review by the courts. The OEC has wide powers to require the production of information and documentation and, upon finding a breach of the Act, can require offending agreements or conduct to be brought to an end and may impose fines.

An action for unfair competition can be brought before the courts. Otherwise anti-competitive practices must be brought before the OEC except consumer fraud (ie misleading statements) where there is dual jurisdiction.

It should be noted in passing that the Fixing of Prices Act (Act LXXVII) permits direct intervention by the government in fixing prices where the provisions in the Competition Act are not sufficient to prevent the harmful restriction of competition and abuse of economic superiority.

CONCESSIONS

Both the Hungarian Constitution and the Civil Code contain the concept of exclusive property of the state – for example, minerals, rivers, waterways, roads and railways. However, there may be occasions where the state or local government wishes to allow a private sector organisation, after having submitted an advantageous offer, to exploit exclusive state property. This concept is contained in the Concessions Act (Act XVI of 1991).

The following fall within this Act:

- national public roads and roadworks, railways, canals, sewerage (including main agricultural water utilities), ports, public airports and regional utilities;

- basic telecommunication networks and the frequencies used for telecommunication;

- public electric power stations and the national electric power transmission network;

- local public roads and their roadworks constituting the assets of local authorities and local public utilities;

- mining exploration and exploitation;

- transport and storage of products by pipelines;

- production and sale of fossil fuels and nuclear substances;

- production and the sale of drugs and similar materials;

- organisation and operation of gambling;

- basic postal services (letter-post and cash remittance);

- telecommunication services (public telephones, mobile radio telephones, paging systems and other data transmissions, broadcasting services and distribution of radio and television programmes) but excluding closed-circuit broadcasting services;

- passenger and goods transport on railways; and

- scheduled passenger transport on public roads.

The activities set down above can be carried out either by a state-owned company or economic entity or by a private sector person or company temporarily given the right to exercise the state monopoly over the activity by a concession contract.

Concession contracts are open to anyone, both residents and non-residents. The award of the concession contract is by way of tender and the tender is open to anyone, unless the interests of defence or national security require a restriction upon tenderers to pre-selected invitees. The award of the tender lies with the responsible minister or the council of the local authority as appropriate. The right to carry on the concession may contain a condition that the state will recover the cost of the investment in the concession from the public – for example through road tolls.

The Concession Act determines the most important provisions of the concession contract. The provisions in the Act frequently depart from the general rules of contracts contained in the Civil Code. However, in cases where specific rules are not laid down by the Concession Act, the provisions of the Civil Code will apply.

The basic features of the concession contract are as follows:

- A concession contract may be concluded for a definite period only, not exceeding 35 years. The concession contract may be extended on one occasion for a period no longer than one-half of the original period, without inviting new tenders. The concession contract may only be determined before the end of the concession period in accordance with the Act – namely, for breach of conditions of tender; where the successful tenderer has failed to establish a resident business association to exploit the concession within 90 days of signing the contract; and due to revocation of any licence or permission authorising the activity which is the subject of the concession.

- A concession may be granted for a fee or in return for the provision of services, as may be agreed between the parties.

- The concession having been granted, the person under-taking the concession activity will be granted a partial market exclusivity during the period fixed in the agreement.

- The concession contract does not affect the property in the asset. If an asset is brought into the concession then ownership of that asset is passed to the state or local authority.

- On the conclusion of the concession contract the state or local authority renounces its public immunity. It can therefore sue or be sued. Legal disputes originating from the concession contract can be settled in a court of law.

International arbitration may be used in disputes where the concession contract is concluded with a non-resident.

The Concession Act states that the person or organisation concluding the concession contract must establish a business association registered in Hungary within 90 days of signing the concession contract. The Act does not prescribe that the successful tenderer should hold a majority in the concession company, although it is likely that the state or local authority would insist upon this.

If a state licence is required for the concession, this is to be obtained separately before entering into the concession contract. Therefore, the concession company can only exercise its activity when it possesses the requisite licence. The case of withdrawal of the licence itself does not automatically result in the determination of the concession contract (although the contract may require this). However, if the concession company becomes insolvent the concession contract is determined.

17

Employment Law

SJ Berwin & Co

CONSTITUTIONAL GUARANTEES

The Hungarian Constitution contains some basic rights on employment:

- everyone has the right to work, to free choice of employment and occupation;
- everyone has the right to equal pay for equal work without discrimination;
- everyone who works has the right to earnings corresponding to the amount and quality of work;
- everyone has the right to leisure time and regular paid holidays;
- legislation will ensure protection for women and young people in their employment;
- everyone has the right to form with others an organisation for the protection of economic and social rights;
- the right to strike may be exercised within the framework of the law that regulates it, which to be passed requires a two-thirds majority of MPs; and
- the Hungarian Republic must make arrangements for health and safety at work.

THE LABOUR CODE

The legal provisions relating to the employer/employee relationship are in the Labour Code (Act XXII of 1992). The Code applies to all employment in Hungary, to employees of Hungarian employers working abroad and to Hungarian carriers except:

- the civil service;
- the holders of elected or other office;
- where the employer is a foreign state or diplomatic mission; and
- where the employer and the employee are the citizens of the same foreign state – therefore a British company employing a British employee in Hungary will not be bound by the Code, but a British company employing a Hungarian employee or indeed a German employee will be.

The Labour Code, as with the Civil Code, contains certain provisions that are mandatory and others that are dispositive. Dispositive provisions of the Code may be expressly excluded by agreement but, if not so expressly excluded, will apply.

There are some general provisions relating to employment contained in the Labour Code:

- The employer, factory council and employees must co-operate in the course of exercising rights and fulfilling obligations. The employer may only disclose personal details of an employee as required by law or with the employee's consent.

- During the period of employment the employee must not, unless authorised by law, behave in a manner that might pose a threat to his employer's rightful business interest.

- The rights and duties specified in the Code must be exercised in accordance with their purpose. The exercise of a right is not proper if it aims or leads to the curtailment of the rightful interest of others or harassment or suppression of opinion.

- Unless a law specifically states otherwise, there are no general formalities for legal statements relating to employment. A mistake by one party which ought to have been recognised by the other invalidates any agreement. A person entering into an agreement under undue influence may contest the validity of that agreement within 30 days.

- An agreement which violates the law is void. An employee

may not in advance relinquish rights which guarantee
wages or curtail other rights to his detriment.

- Rights and obligations arising from an invalid agreement
  shall be treated as valid.

- The limitation period for claims relating to employment is
  three years.

- Collective agreements may not violate the law.

- There is a prohibition against discrimination for employment on the grounds of sex, age, nationality, race, country
  of origin, religion, participation in federations and political
  views.

Separate provisions in the Code apply to employees in executive
positions; for example they are not bound by collective agreements.

EMPLOYMENT

Terms of employment

A person who has completed his compulsory school education
may become an employee. A minor under 16 years of age
requires the consent of his guardian to enter employment. A
woman or minor (under 18) may not be employed in work that
may be physically detrimental to them.

Contracts of employment cannot be contrary to the Labour
Code, nor can any collective agreement (as explained below) be
entered into with a trade union unless it contains more
favourable terms for the employee.

The Civil Code imposes two mandatory terms in contracts of
employment – the basic wage payable to the employee and the
employee's official duties and place of work. Other terms may be
incorporated by agreement, and the provisions negotiated and
contained in collective agreements (covering such areas as
working hours, shifts and periods of notice) may be incorporated
within the employee's contract of employment by way of
reference.

Contracts of employment must be in writing (unless they are
for a period not exceeding five days). Only an employee may
claim invalidity of a contract not being in writing and he must do
so within 30 days of commencing work. In the absence of

agreement to the contrary the contract of employment is for an indefinite period. The duration of a definite period may not exceed five years and employment for a definite period converts into an indefinite period if the employee works (with the knowledge of his employer) one day following the expiration of the period. Employment for 30 days or less will only be extended by the original period. The contract of employment may stipulate a trial period of 30 days, but collective agreements may extend or reduce this with a maximum duration of 3 months. Either party may determine the contract during the trial period with immediate effect. The employer and the employee may only vary the contract of employment by consent.

Termination of contracts of employment

A contract of employment automatically ceases upon:

- the death of the employee;
- the employer ceasing to exist; or
- the expiry of a fixed-term contract.

A contract of employment may be determined:

- by mutual consent at any time;
- by ordinary notice; or
- by extraordinary notice.

A fixed-term contract of employment may only be determined early by mutual consent, extraordinary notice or, where the contract so states, at the end of a trial period. The employer may determine a fixed-term contract if he pays the wages to the employee up to the end of the fixed term.

Ordinary notice is defined as being at least 30 days, increasing by reference to years of service up to a maximum of 60 days after 20 years employment. Such notice may be given by the employer or employee. However, where notice of dismissal is given by the employer it must be substantiated. The reason for the dismissal must be connected with the employee's competence, conduct or the employer's operations. Where dismissal is because of incompetence or conduct, the employee must be given an opportunity to defend himself. An employer may not dismiss an employee (i) during or within 30 days of sick leave (for a maximum period of one year or the entire duration following an accident at work); (ii) during the statutory permitted period for nursing children or a sick relative, and during pregnancy or six months after birth; (iii) during military service; and (iv) during the 5 years up to pensionable age unless there is a justifiable reason. The employee must be relieved of his duties for at least half of the notice period.

Where an employee is dismissed by ordinary notice he is entitled to severance pay (except where the employee is eligible for a pension). The amount of severance pay is calculated by reference to monthly pay over years service, with a minimum of one month's pay for 3 years service and a maximum of six months' pay for 25 or more years service.

Extraordinary notice may be given by either employer or employee where the other party:

- is in breach of his obligations arising from the employment either intermittently or by virtue of gross negligence (any collective agreement must define the categories of behaviour to come within this head); or

- by virtue of his conduct makes the employment impossible to continue.

Extraordinary notice must be given within 30 days of ascertaining the facts giving rise to such notice, within 6 months of the occurrence of the event giving rise to the notice and within one year of the breach of a collective agreement provision. Where extraordinary notice is given the provisions applicable to ordinary notice do not apply. If such notice is given by an employer the employee is due wages to which he would have been entitled if ordinary notice had been given.

Where a court determines that an employer has determined an employee's employment unlawfully, the employee must, if he so wishes, be reinstated. In addition to this, he is entitled to lost wages and compensation for losses incurred. If the employer does not wish to re-employ the employee or the employee does not wish reinstatement then the court may waive reinstatement and instead order the payment of twice the severance payable to the employee if ordinary notice had been given. If the employee is not entitled to severance pay he must be paid two months' wages. Alternative compensation does not apply to the dismissal, whether by ordinary or extraordinary notice, if it breaches the provisions prohibiting discrimination on notice (ie pregnancy, etc).

If an employee fails to determine his contract of employment in accordance with the Labour Code he is liable to pay compensation to the employer calculated by reference to years of service, but not to exceed 1.5 months' wages.

Working practices

The employer has several obligations to the employee as set down in the Labour Code:

- to employ the employee in accordance with his contract of employment;
- to ensure the employee's health and safety at work;
- to organise the work in such a way that the employee can meet his obligations;
- to provide the employee with information and guidance to carry out his work; and
- to pay the employee wages due to him in accordance with the contract of employment.

For his part the employee also has obligations to the employer under the Labour Code:

- to attend his place of work fit to undertake his duties;
- to undertake his work in a professional manner;
- to co-operate with his fellow workers;
- to fulfil his duties personally;
- to undertake his work in accordance with his contract of employment and the employer's lawful instructions;
- to safeguard his employer's business secrets;
- to attend any training or education course provided by his employer (at the employer's cost);
- to undertake work outside of his official duties or away from the usual place of business where this is reasonable; and
- to inform his employer if he obtains additional employment (the employer may prohibit this).

The Labour Code also contains provisions covering hours of work and leisure time. The working day is 8 hours, which may be extended by regulations or by agreement, but so as not to exceed 12 hours. In particularly hazardous work, legislation or a collective agreement may restrict the number of hours to six. There is also an exception to the maximum hours for seasonal work. The arrangement of working hours is established by a collective agreement or, in the absence of such, as may be specified by the employer. There is an express prohibition against employing women on night work during pregnancy and until the child is at least one year old.

The Code also contains provisions governing leave. These cover illness (up to a maximum of 10 days annually including accident at work), maternity leave (24 weeks), unpaid leave for looking after a child until the child is one year old, unpaid leave not exceeding 30 days or up to one year if it is for building the employee's own house, military service, unpaid leave for nursing a sick relative and annual leave. Guaranteed approved leave depends upon the age of the employee, with a minimum of 20 days and up to a maximum of 30 when the employee reaches 45. An employee under 18 is entitled to an additional 5 days leave and an employee responsible for looking after children is also entitled to 2, 4 or 7 additional days leave depending upon the number of children. Disabled persons and persons with particularly hazardous jobs are also entitled to additional leave. Allocation of leave depends on the employer. The Code also covers other working arrangements such as work breaks (20 minutes after 6 hours and after 3 consecutive hours of overtime, and 11 hours between work periods and two days off a week, one of which must be Sunday) and public holidays (1 January, 15 March, Easter Monday, 1 May, Whitsun Monday, 20 August, 23 October and 25–26 December).

Wages

An employee is entitled to wages on the basis of his contract of employment. An employee must receive a personal wage but may also receive performance-related pay. A supplement is payable for night work and afternoon shifts or work on a rest day or public holiday. There is a system set up by the government of mandatory minimum wages within different fields of employment.

Wages must be paid in Hungarian forints and without deduction unless the law states otherwise. If the law permits payment in kind, such must not exceed 20 per cent of the wage. The Code contains rules relating to methods of paying wages.

Compensation

An employee is liable for damage caused by a breach of his employment obligations. Where damage arises from negligence, the amount of compensation shall not exceed 50 per cent of a month's wages. Full compensation is due for wilful damage or loss of employer's equipment on loan to the employee.

An employer is fully liable for damage to an employee arising in connection with the employment, regardless of fault, unless the employer proves the damage was caused by an unavoidable cause outside the employer's control or to the employee's own reprehensible conduct. The employer is also responsible for loss or damage to the employee's property but he can specify where the employee's property is to be stored.

LABOUR RELATIONS

The Code guarantees freedom of organisation and participation in protection of work conditions. Both employers and employees have the right to form representative organisations. The government has a duty to co-operate and intervene in matters of national significance to labour relations including:

- mass redundancies;
- the minimum wage;
- maximum work time; and
- national wage negotiations.

For the purposes of the Code, an employee organisation which has as its primary function the development and protection of employee interests is a trade union. Trade unions have various rights:

- to operate a branch in any company;
- to inform members of their rights as to working conditions;
- to conclude a collective agreement;

- to request information from the employer on issues relating to employees' employment;

- to verify compliance with workplace regulations; and

- to object to unlawful action by the employer (and to apply to the courts if consultation fails).

Trade union officials are allowed paid, reduced, working hours. An employee's employment must not be dependent upon trade union membership and an employee may not be dismissed for trade union activities.

Collective agreements are entered into between employers and trade unions and regulate rights and obligations arising from employment and relations between parties to the contract. Only one collective agreement is to be concluded with each employer. Employees are obliged to follow the terms of a collective agreement. The agreement may be determined by 3 months notice after 6 months. Finally, all employers with more than 50 employees must have a Factory Council. All employees have the right to participate in and elect the Factory Council. Detailed procedures are set down in the Code. The employee must consult the Factory Council on proposals for:

- measures affecting large groups of employees;

- maintaining personal records;

- employee training;

- retraining employees;

- allocating annual leave;

- inaugurating new work methods;

- internal work regulations; and

- tenders accompanied by financial reward.

The agreement of the Council is necessary for safety regulations and the use of welfare monies. The employer must inform the Council of major business decisions and decisions concerning wages and earnings.

In the case of labour disputes, there are consultation arrangements giving a seven-day 'cooling off' period. The parties may seek mediation or arbitration to resolve the dispute. Breaches of employment obligations are dealt with as a legal dispute before the courts.

FOREIGN LABOUR

Work permits

Every foreign employee must apply for a work permit at the Labour Office of the relevant local authority except:

- where a treaty between Hungary and the state of the person concerned dispenses with this requirement;

- diplomatic staff;

- artists, teachers and scientists in certain circumstances;

- persons employed to start up businesses and persons employed by foreign persons to undertake repair work pursuant to a guarantee;

- settled refugees; and

- the staff of representative or information offices of foreign persons.

The permit is valid for one year, but may be extended.

An employer can apply for an outline permit which is valid for three months. This outline permit will set out the proposed employment of foreign persons. Within this period, the Labour Office is obliged to give permits to any number of applicants for the jobs indicated in the outline.

Sections of the labour market are reserved for Hungarian nationals. There is a general reservation that a foreigner cannot obtain employment if there are Hungarian workers with appropriate qualifications. There are also some posts reserved exclusively to Hungarian citizens – for example, elected officers, judges, etc.

SOCIAL INSURANCE PAYMENTS AND PENSIONS

In 1991 all employers had to pay 43 per cent of each employee's earnings as a social insurance payment and employees had to contribute 10 per cent of their earnings.

Every person who contributes to the social insurance fund has the right to a pension. The amount of pension is determined by the years of service and the worker's earnings during the three years prior to retirement. The minimum is 33 per cent (for 10 years service) and the maximum is 75 per cent (for 42 years or more service) of the average amount of the employee's earnings during the previous three years. There is a current minimum pension for 1991 of Ft5200.

Only a few people are not entitled to receive a pension. For example, self-employed persons who do not pay social insurance contributions or employed persons who do not fulfil the minimum 10-year requirement. The employer is obliged to retain social insurance payments from his employee's earnings and pays this sum, together with his contribution, to the government.

18

The Labour Market

KPMG Peat Marwick

The success of any business venture depends to a large extent on finding competent and motivated staff. In Hungary, as in the rest of Central and Eastern Europe, demand outstrips supply.

POPULATION AND LABOUR FORCE

Since 1981 Hungary has been losing about 20,000 people per year. Hungary is the only country in Europe which is experiencing negative population growth rates: the population is declining at the rate of 0.2 per cent a year as the result of ageing, high mortality rates and very low birthrates. The active population is estimated to be 5.4 million out of a total population of 10.6 million. Labour force employment by sectors is shown in Tables 18.1 and 18.2.

Table 18.1 *Active population by sector*

	1980	1990	1991
Agriculture	21.0	18.8	18.4
Industry	41.2	38.0	37.4
Services	37.8	43.2	44.2

Source: Central Statistical Office.

Traditionally, employees were guaranteed a job for life by the state but, at the same time, initiative was discouraged. Guaranteed employment of each citizen resulted in overstaffing of all organisations. Pay levels were controlled by the state and pay differentials were low compared to those found in the West. The differential ratio between a senior manager and a skilled worker

Table 18.2   *Active earners by social sector (in %), 1991*

	State	Private
Industry	89	11
Building Construction	72	28
Trade	71	29

Source: Hungarian Statistical Yearbook.

was about 3 to 1 in 1980. Another important characteristic was the 'second' economy. To make ends meet, many Hungarians supplemented their income with secondary jobs and other sideline activities. This meant long hours of work but little inclination or incentive to work hard for the main (state) employer. This resulted in inefficient use of labour, low productivity and underemployment.

Managers usually lacked exposure to the end-users of their products and to the world economy generally. They were not required to make decisions, take responsibility, prioritise goals or solve problems, and this antipathy to enterprise culture is still perpetuated in many state-owned enterprises. Older managers may resist new work practices and may not have the ability to motivate staff.

Wages

According to the Central Statistical Office, gross wages grew by 18.1 per cent in the first quarter of 1993 and net wages by 15.5 per cent, compared with a rate of inflation of 24.7 per cent. The minimum salary was set at Ft9000 per month (approximately £60.00) and average wages represent a fifth of West European rates. To this must be added substantial social security costs to cover state insurance and unemployment benefit. There are increasing differences between enterprises – a trilingual secretary employed by a foreign company can expect to earn more than Ft60,000 a month, which is twice as much as an engineer in a state-owned company. Regional differences are also appearing. As most private sector jobs have been created in Budapest, competition is fiercer there than in the rest of the country for qualified staff.

Salaries for senior managers are catching up quickly with those of their Western counterparts. There is a growing trend towards using local managers as joint ventures mature and self-

Table 18.3   *Gross monthly average wages in various sectors of industry (in forints), first quarter 1993*

	Manual	Non-manual
Agriculture	13,440	25,047
Mining	26,433	44,234
Metallurgy	21,113	34,192
Chemical industry	23,847	40,946
Food industry	19,089	34,519
Construction	16,051	32,975
Teaching	14,079	24,456

Source: Hungarian Statistical Monthly Bulletin.

reliance becomes the norm. However, highly qualified managerial talent is in demand and therefore competition is fierce. Managers in Budapest tend to be 10–40 per cent more expensive than in the rest of the country and there are increasing differentials in relation to the size of the joint ventures and the performance of individual managers.

Unemployment

Unemployment was virtually unknown at the end of the 1980s, but now the level is above the European average. Unemployment has been growing rapidly. Between December 1990 and December 1991, the rate of increase was 410 per cent. Rates vary from region to region but the average is 13 per cent. However, the unemployed represented only 3 per cent of the labour force in Budapest, 6 per cent in the west but more than 20 per cent in the north-east (in the Miskolc region). The main cause of unemployment has been restructuring of heavy industry with layoffs in most enterprises totalling up to one-third of their work-force over the past two years. Unemployment was until recently not considered a priority by the government. However, unemployment is causing a social crisis. A solidarity fund has been set up in order to provide a safety net.

EDUCATION AND SKILLS

School is compulsory for children between the ages of 6 and 16. Around 90 per cent continue into higher education (there are 56 universities and colleges in Hungary). In 1984 7 per cent of the adult population had had a university education. Hungary can boast a strong scientific tradition and a number of Nobel prizes – in medicine A Szent-Györgyi, in physics L Szilard and E Teller, and in mathematics Von Neumann.

In the technical and manufacturing areas, the work-force is usually very highly skilled (lack of supplies and machinery meant that innovative solutions had to be found to keep the factory going). However, the very narrow confines and special-isation of vocational training means that specific skills are unadapted to a changing labour market and heavy demand from new sectors such as banking, insurance and tourism will be difficult to meet. More emphasis will need to be placed on developing support skills and functions such as marketing, purchasing and accounting.

Vocational training

With the prospect of serious structural unemployment, attention has concentrated on devising proactive employment measures, such as adult training and retraining schemes. Hungary is the country furthest advanced in developing new legislative and financial frameworks for higher education, with substantial World Bank and some PHARE involvement. The experience of Hungary may prove interesting to other countries in the region, which are faced with the legacy of overspecialised and seg-mented structures that are ill-adapted to new demands.

FINDING THE RIGHT PEOPLE

Recruitment methods are the same as in the West – advertise-ments, word of mouth and headhunting. As the labour market develops, the selection process is becoming more rigorous. Finding a good secretary with more than a passing knowledge of English, a sales manager with a knowledge of the local market or an accountant to deal with cost and tax matters can be difficult, particularly in Budapest where competition for a relatively small pool of qualified employees is fierce. Larger pools, in particular for specialist engineers and technicians, lie beyond Budapest in the regional cities of Gyor, Debrecen or Pécs where recruitment and retention costs are lower. And as the infrastructure improves, the importance of Budapest's central location will decrease.

Former Foreign Trade Organisations are a good source of people with language skills and knowledge of Western ways. However, flexibility should be preferred to direct relevant experience. Placing advertisements in a newspaper is an effective way of finding the right person (especially if they are written in English), particularly for engineering, manufacturing and sales positions. For specialised positions, some trade publications carry recruitment sections, but this approach can be time-consuming and requires a good knowledge of local market conditions. Foreign companies dominate the market for search and selection. These are often used to hunt for the best candidates for management, finance and accounting positions, especially when the requirements are very specialised.

Local universities and business schools are an obvious source of young talent. Institutes now hold recruitment fairs. Generally, students speak another foreign language – usually English, French or German. Young people lack experience but they are not tarnished by the uncompetitive working practices of their elders and they are keen to learn (although they may also be more likely to leave if dissatisfied with pay levels).

Be prepared to offer a good level of training. This is particularly true in sales and marketing where it is difficult to find people with directly relevant expertise and experience. The improvement of work-force attitudes, performance and motivation is a fundamental issue that will need to be resolved. Transferring corporate know-how demands considerable hard work, whether in an acquisition or a greenfield investment.

Benefits can prove strong incentives – a car is attractive but expensive as it is fully taxable and subject to social security costs. The opportunity to travel, career prospects and a training element are also good incentives.

INDUSTRIAL RELATIONS

Unions are likely to have an influence on a foreign company's relations with its employees. There used to be a requirement for employers to establish trade unions but this does not apply to newly formed companies. However, when managing layoffs in an acquisition it is important to work with them, since they can be obstructive if not involved. Trade unions are still undergoing a process of restructuring. Their mood is generally non-militant.

Half-a-dozen organisations claim to represent employees, but they maintain very tense or non-existent relationships with each other, which has prevented them from presenting a common front. The old official unions have survived under a new umbrella organisation (MSZOSZ) but they have lost their monopolistic status and the crucial role they used to play in the decision-making process of enterprises. Industrial action is generally sporadic and uncoordinated. More widely publicised are the actions of groups of individuals, usually self-employed, against government policy.

19

The Environment

SJ Berwin & Co

Following the end of World War II the social and economic structure of Hungary changed dramatically. Hungary has undergone an era of rapid industrialisation and urbanisation, initially without regard to the environmental consequences. Although significant problems exist, they are not considered as serious as the 'black triangle' where Poland, the Czech Republic and the Slovak Republics meet the former East Germany.

Hungary receives assistance from the West to meet its environmental problems. The key environmental issues facing the country today are:

- air pollution, particularly by sulphur dioxide as coal is the primary fuel;

- water pollution due to lack of pollution abatement equipment and inadequate waste water treatment plants; and

- waste disposal and contaminated land.

Hungarian industry is dominated by the production of iron, steel, aluminium and cement. In addition there are a considerable number of chemical, textile and synthetic material production plants. Hungary's reliance on loans from the West has gradually increased since 1980. It became a member of the IMF and World Bank in 1982 and it is usual for loans from these organisations to contain environmental protection provisions which have helped Hungary become aware of the need to increase its environmental protection standards. This is also an important factor to take into account should Hungary eventually succeed in its application to become a member of the EC.

AIR POLLUTION

The rapid growth of industrialisation without concern for the environmental consequences has led to a significant deterioration in air quality throughout Hungary, particularly concentrated in the industrial areas and cities. One of the main causes of pollution is the production of electricity from coal-powered stations. Coal is the primary fuel and as Hungary has no black coal reserves, it must rely on its brown and lignite coal reserves which have a high sulphur content. Coal burning is the main source of sulphur and dust pollution. Power plants are believed to be responsible for 40 per cent of sulphur dioxide emissions, and the lignite-burning Gagarain power plant is recognised as the largest single source.

At present there are proposals to introduce legislation to require the installation of sulphur emission control equipment in power stations, and feasibility studies are being carried out on three existing power plants funded under the EC's PHARE programme.

Dust emissions from cement works, iron and steel industries are also a source of pollution, while the increased use of cars and vehicles is responsible for poor air quality through nitrogen oxide and carbon monoxide emissions.

Despite its problems Hungary has joined European and global programmes to protect the atmosphere. It has agreed to reduce its sulphur dioxide emissions by 3 per cent by 1993, which is equivalent to 1980 levels. It has also signed the Protocol on Nitrogen Oxide Emissions and agreed to reduce these by 31 December 1994 to the equivalent of 1987 levels. Hungary has joined the Vienna Convention on the Protection of the Stratosphere and agreed to reduce the use of ozone depleting substances such as halons and freons.

WATER POLLUTION

Like many Western countries, Hungary's water quality continues to deteriorate. Surface waters are at risk from both industrial and municipal effluents as there is little or no investment to improve existing sewage treatment works or construct new ones.

The increased use of fertilisers and pesticides and the intensification of agricultural methods has also caused surface water quality to deteriorate. Ground water resources are at risk especially from mining-related contamination and lechates from waste disposal sites.

Although water pollution does not receive the same level of attention as air pollution, opposition to the Nagymaros Dam was partly based on the effects on water quality which could arise from the reduced river flows following the construction of the dam. The project originated in the 1960s (being implemented by both the Hungarian and Czechoslovak governments) and involved the construction of a barrage system to utilise the Danube for the production of electric power, inland navigation and the management of water supplies. The Gabcikovo Barrage, a diversion canal and most of the Dunakiliti Reservoir would be situated in Czechoslovakia, while the Dunakiliti Weir, a smaller part of the reservoir and the Nagymaros Barrage would be situated in Hungary. The Dunakiliti Reservoir would collect and store water for further use, and the diversion canal would provide sufficient water for the Gabcikovo Power Plant. The Nagymaros Barrage would compensate the water flows released by the Gabcikovo Power Plant and would also involve the construction of a smaller power plant to serve Hungary.

As negotiations between both governments continued, culminating in the signing of an international agreement, the Hungarian public became concerned about the implications of the project because it failed to consider or address the potential effects on the environment and natural resources (particularly as 45 per cent of Hungary's drinking water supply comes from the percolated water in the area of the Gabcikovo-Nagymaros Barrage system). Following public protests, the Hungarian government asked the Czechoslovak government to suspend work pending further research into the environmental implications of the project. The Czechoslovak government refused and the construction works at Nagymaros ceased in 1989. The Hungarian government terminated the agreement unilaterally in 1992 and construction is unlikely to resume.

WASTE DISPOSAL

There are few controls over the supervision and management of waste and only hazardous waste is regulated. It is believed that only 275 waste disposal sites are licensed out of a total of 2600.

The development of low waste technologies is in its infancy because there is little or no investment in this area. There are no tax concessions or incentives to encourage recycling or re-use so most waste is dumped in landfill sites. In view of the lack of controls over the management of waste, there is concern about the risk to ground water supplies and soil contamination by lechates from waste disposal sites and from methane generation.

NATURE CONSERVATION

Land allocated for nature conservation purposes is the least affected by industrial pollution. In the 1960s, the former National Office for Nature Conservation established areas for nature conservation purposes in response to public fears over the protection of natural habitats and species. Approximately 7 per cent of the total land area (600,000 hectares) has been allocated for conservation purposes, which include 183 protected areas of national significance, 4 national parks and 900 areas of local significance. No less than 619 animal species are protected.

LEGAL STRUCTURE

Although legislation with the specific aim of protecting the environment was not introduced in Hungary until 1976, environmental provisions could be found in no less than 500 legal measures.

The 1976 Act On the Protection of the Human Environment is the primary legislative instrument dealing with the environment, and it provided the impetus for the subsequent reorganisation of administrative bodies to achieve a more centralised approach to environmental protection. The 1976 Act sets out a number of environmental objectives that are supported by the use of criminal sanctions.

Chapter I deals with the fundamental principles of environmental policy:

- the protection of the human environment is in the interest and duty of Hungarian society;

- every citizen has the right to live in a healthy environment; and

- the state, companies, co-operatives, social organisations and citizens must observe environmental legislation.

Section 4 then describes the tasks of environmental protection:

- the promotion and protection of the human environment;

- the recognition of causes of pollution; and

- the establishment of methods and conditions to prevent, reduce or remove pollution.

Chapter II contains detailed provisions aimed at protecting the environment. It is divided into different sections dealing with specific sectors: land, water, air, nature conservation, landscape and the built environment (referred to as the human environment).

Land

Only the management, transportation, disposal and importation of hazardous waste is regulated. Penalties for failing to comply with the legislation are severe – for example a fine of Ft100,000 for each tonne of waste material imported without a licence can be imposed and, in addition, the importer may be ordered to return or destroy the waste at its own cost. In cases of severe risk of pollution, the regulatory authorities can order the activities responsible for the production of waste to stop.

Water

The contamination and pollution of surface and ground waters is prohibited. The construction of factories or other facilities must include the provision of appropriate sewage treatment equipment as required by other statutory regulations. The Act also contains general provisions dealing with the maintenance of water supplies, the establishment of protected areas to maintain the quality and quantity of drinking water, and the use of plant equipment to prevent flooding.

Air

The harmful pollution of the air is prohibited, and applications to construct factories and other facilities (eg mining, industrial, building or agricultural activities) must include appropriate air emission abatement equipment. Existing factories are required to reduce or eliminate the amount of pollutants emitted in accordance with statutory provisions. The manufacture, importation, selling and operation of fuels, motor vehicles, machines, heating and other equipment which cause air pollution in breach of the specified regulations is prohibited. The Act authorises the establishment of regions of priority protection to restrict harmful emissions.

Penalties

Chapter III describes penalties that can be imposed where the provisions of the Act are breached. In most cases the legislation is enforced by the use of criminal sanctions. For example, Section 44 provides that anyone who carries out activities in breach of the 1976 Act will be liable to pay a fine which will be assessed in accordance with a level of harm or damage caused as a result of those activities. (The fine could be substantial if it represents the cost of clean-up operations.)

The increased awareness of environmental issues has been reflected in the level of fines awarded since 1976 which have increased from Ft200,000 per year to over Ft2 billion per year. In addition, the responsible person may be held personally liable and ordered to pay a fine or imprisoned. The Act contains powers enabling the regulatory authorities to restrict polluting activities or, if necessary, close the factory.

Problems associated with air pollution have received more attention than other sectors. In addition to the provisions contained in the 1976 Act, legislation has been passed allocating different air quality standards to certain territories. For example, designated nature conservation areas and holiday resorts are the highest category (and therefore experience the strictest controls) whereas industrial and large-scale agricultural areas not situated adjacent to conurbations or nature conservation areas have been allocated lower air quality standards.

New projects, or the alteration or extension of existing projects, must satisfy the emission criteria for the area where they are located and this may involve the provision of appropriate pollution abatement equipment. Operators are required by law to provide regulatory bodies with copies of monitoring data and failure to comply is a criminal offence, although provisions exist enabling fines awarded for breaches involving the cement, metallurgy or electricity industries to be reduced (even though these are recognised as some of the most polluting industries).

Emissions from vehicles, aircraft and all forms of public transport (rail and buses) are also regulated.

Future developments

Although the January 1987 system of air quality regulation is largely responsible for the improvement in air quality, it does not provide any standards governing emissions of pollutants from power plants, which are responsible for the largest source of pollutants. In recognition of the need to introduce stricter controls, the government has announced a series of proposals to require:

- the reduction in emissions of pollutants from power plants, chemical factories and other industrial plants;

- the introduction of catalytic converters on vehicles to reduce nitrogen dioxide, carbon monoxide and hydrocarbon emissions;

- the introduction of low waste technologies and technologies for the re-use of wastes;

- additional legislation to ensure the safe disposal of hazardous waste including the provision of new waste disposal sites and incinerators.

In the area of waste pollution control, the government's proposals include the improvement of waste water and sewage treatment plants, the use of new technologies to deal with effluent from paper mills, manufacturing plants and cellulose manufacturing plants, and general improvements to drinking water quality.

Integrated pollution control

No legislation exists which is equivalent to the integrated pollution control provisions contained in the UK's Environment Protection Act 1990. The impact on each sector of the environment is considered independently.

Administration of environmental law

The Council of Ministers is responsible for the formulation and introduction of environmental legislation, and the Ministry for Environmental Protection and Water Management, established in 1987, is the central government body primarily responsible for the enforcement of environmental legislation and the development of environmental policy. The Ministry is responsible for the co-ordination and harmonisation of all activities relating to environmental protection and water management.

The administration and enforcement of environmental legislation is patchy, as several other ministries (eg the Ministry for Social and Health Affairs, the Ministry of Agriculture and Food and the Ministry for Construction and Settlement Development) are also responsible for elements of environmental protection. In addition, 12 Inspectorates of Environmental Protection and Water Management are responsible for enforcing legislation previously handled by county and local authorities.

Enforcement of environmental legislation

Generally speaking, the enforcement of environmental legislation is patchy. Existing establishments that produce goods at fixed prices (eg steam mills) or that have a monopoly on their produce (eg power plants) have not been very sensitive to fines as they can be cheaper than the cost of installing up-to-date pollution abatement equipment. Despite this, the level of fines has increased dramatically and factories have been closed down where the activities pose a high risk to human health or the environment.

GUIDELINES FOR INVESTORS

Potential investors in Hungary should be aware of environmental concerns from two aspects. First, those involved in the acquisition of, or joint venture with, existing businesses must consider the cost of installing pollution abatement equipment in order to achieve the increasingly stringent legislative requirements.

The second aspect concerns the opportunities that may arise out of the need to protect the environment – for example a number of key industrial sectors have been identified with potential for investment from an environmental prospective:

- *Energy*: The energy sector has been identified by the US Department of Commerce as a potential source of Western investment with opportunities in coal-burning technologies in the short term and alternative energy uses such as solar and wind energy in the long term. The use of cleaner forms of energy, such as natural gas, is expected to increase.

- *Chemicals*: Hungary has a significant chemical sector and over 50 per cent is energy related (oil refining, gas production and distribution). Oil desulphurisation capacities have increased in response to stricter environmental controls. The pharmaceutical industry is responsible for a significant proportion of exports.

- *Paper*: The paper and cellulose industries are significant contributors to water pollution and waste problems and have been specifically targeted in the government's proposals to require the increased use of pollution abatement equipment.

- *Vehicles*: Foreign manufacturers such as Suzuki are proposing to produce vehicles in Hungary to replace the notorious Trabant. The Hungarian government is pursuing the possibility of clean-up equipment for two-stroke vehicles although the research is complicated.

- *Pollution abatement equipment*: The US Department of Commerce believes that considerable opportunities exist for Western firms to invest in the production, manufacture and supply of pollution abatement equipment in Hungary. Specific sectors identified are air emissions, waste water treatment and low waste technologies. Considerable international funding is available for clean-up operations.

Further advice

In addition to the government agencies described above, the Regional Environment Centre for Central and Eastern Europe, located in Budapest, may provide additional information. This body is an independent, non-profit organisation supported by the governments of Hungary, the United States, the EC, and the Netherlands. The main purposes are to:

- collect and disseminate environmental information;

- develop an environmental database on Eastern Europe; and

- act as a clearing house to match the needs of the region with world-wide expertise and resources in environmental technology and clean-up.

The Centre will concentrate on three vital areas:

- impacts on health caused by environmental degradation;

- inclusion of less reliance on pollution control in favour of more cost-effective pollution prevention; and

- facilitating the adoption of an energy efficiency policy that encourages the use of alternative energy plans and a reduction in current energy levels to support the reduction in pollution levels.

Steps to take

There is a recognised need in Hungary, like other European countries, for environmental technologies and programmes offering maximum long-term gains for minimum short-term costs. Investors should be careful, however, not to offer technologies and approaches that would not be acceptable in the West.

Greens in Hungary have worried that 'third-rate Soviet technology, which poisoned us for 40 years, will now be replaced by second-rate technology from the West sold cheaply to us because it is too polluting for them'. (Zsuzsa Beres of the Hungarian Green Party, in *The Guardian*, 19 January 1990). In response to these concerns, the EC is establishing a code of conduct for investment in Eastern Europe that will take account of environmental issues. Increasingly, environmental regulations in Hungary will also make investment in sub-standard technology too risky for business.

20

Communications

KPMG Peat Marwick

The Hungarian government knows that if it is to attract significant foreign investment, its communications and information network will need to be overhauled. Few companies can function without telephones, facsimile machines, personal computers, databases and transmission networks. In the past, staff at Allami Biztosito, Hungary's biggest insurance company, were reported to load data on to floppy disks and take them by car to processing centres because managers had little faith in Hungary's telephone system. In that respect, the commercial environment in Hungary is quite unlike the West. Personal computers dominated equipment and, in 1992, there were estimated to be 120,000 of them compared to 1,500 minicomputers and 200 mainframes. Even so, the ratio of PCs to white-collar employees was 1/20 against 1/5 in Western Europe and 1/3 in the USA. Lack of cash and political considerations have held back development in this crucial field.

As well as internal restrictions, externally imposed barriers to technological progress were imposed. Through the Co-ordinating Committee on Multilateral Export Controls (CoCom), the NATO countries and Japan restricted exports of advanced Western technology to Eastern Europe on military and political grounds. These controls were eased in June 1990. In May 1992, Hungary was removed from the list of CoCom proscribed countries, following its introduction of satisfactory controls on exports from its territory. This means that although licences may still be necessary, they will not be subject to CoCom procedures.

The Hungarians are not interested in old technology and outmoded Western equipment. Although the telecommunications network is, in many aspects, primitive, the common thinking among Hungarian government officials is that only modern and world class technology will make Hungary competitive.

INFORMATION TECHNOLOGY

Under communist rule, in Hungary (and in Eastern Europe generally) banking and insurance made few demands for new technology. The manufacturing sector was starved of computer-integrated manufacturing and computer-aided design systems. Central planning meant that there was little incentive to invest in new technology in order to improve productivity, increase output and cut costs. However the change in the competitive environment means that existing technology is too inflexible to support business and handle complex transactions.

Hardware

Many small companies dealt mainly in IBM compatible clones and supplied a mixture of products and services, mostly at the low end of the market. Large-scale computers were rarely available, but Hungary was a major producer of copies of the DEC VAX.

After the collapse of communist rule, the market for business information technology systems has become more fragmented and the American computer giants started taking a keen interest in Hungary. Their first move was to invest through joint ventures rather than sell through wholesalers, and they initially concentrated on gaining market share. Hewlett-Packard established a joint venture with Controll in 1991, Unisys-SZUV and Bull Videoton were among the other joint ventures established at the time. Today, most of the big names have bought out their partners to form a wholly-owned subsidiary, sometimes retaining distribution ties with their former partner. Although information is difficult to obtain, in 1992, IBM and DEC seem to have dominated the market.

Software

Whereas, in most Central and East European countries, software piracy is rife, and was encouraged by the authorities in order to avoid the economic and political restrictions placed on obtaining Western technology, Hungary has protected software since 1983. Copyright laws are similar to those in the West and reasonable attempts are made to enforce them. The domestic market is still expanding. Hungarian versions of international software have been or are being developed. There are about 20 big Hungarian firms such as SZKI, Szamalk, KFKI and PSZTI. A few of them enjoy a good international reputation, in particular SZKI which has developed a character recognition software. Szamalk became a private company in 1990 and is now a holding company for 40 subsidiaries. The others have also been privatised or are in the process of being privatised. These big companies have been joined by many small firms established at the beginning of the 1990s. There are still very few foreign companies, apart from EDS and SG2.

Basic software skills are quite common in Hungary, in particular in relation to PCs. The young are computer literate and technically informed. The standards of programming skills are high.

The enormous demand for renewal and creation of information systems, both in the public and private sector, will mean that the market is set to grow in an erratic and volatile way. Public services, education and training have obtained funding from the International Bank for Reconstruction and Development and other international institutions.

TELECOMMUNICATIONS

As elsewhere in the region, the telecommunications network suffers from low penetration, low completion rates, poor line quality and obsolete switching and transmission equipment. Waiting for a line to be installed used to take well over a decade on average. The fixed network needs modernising and in many cases rebuilding. Despite the old technology, the networks are well maintained and provided they are not overloaded function reasonably well, but data transmission at speeds over 300 bps may be problematic.

CoCom restrictions were relaxed in June 1990. This cut down red tape and eased the sale of equipment to Warsaw Pact countries, bringing about a sense of closer cultural connections with the rest of Europe. The immediate need in order to spur economic growth is to build a better infrastructure for businesses and to provide them with voice and fax lines, direct dialling and international trunk calls. Hungary is equipping itself at a rapid pace. Monetel and Alcatel won tenders to install card and coin operated public telephones. The development of the network has been kept separate from the operation of lines. Ericsson and Siemens won the contract to develop lines over the next five years, but each year they have to compete against each other for the share of the lines planned for the next year. In 1992 Siemens won two-thirds of the installation rights while, in 1993, Ericsson was due to install 200,000 of the planned 300,000 lines.

The right approach on how to operate the lines, though, is still far from clear. Telecommunications and politics are, as in many other countries, entwined. The aims are ambitious – from 15 lines per 100 people at the moment (although the spread is uneven as Budapest with only 20 per cent of the population gets 49 per cent of the share) to 30 by 1996. An affordable and universal service provision implies subsidies of rural residential areas by more profitable services. On the other hand, higher tariffs are needed to make investment attractive. In 1990 Contel won a licence which was later revoked because the Hungarian authorities felt that the published tariffs were too high. It has also warned companies bidding for the GSM cellular network that they should set affordable prices, before changing its mind and deciding to auction the licences to the highest bidder. The socially desirable need for higher penetration requires more than a strictly commercial approach.

Privatisation

Now Hungary plans to privatise its telephone utility. It is the combination of regulatory and market conditions that makes the entry into a new market worthwhile. Foreign operators need to yield a minimum revenue per line or a market share which is sizeable enough to make investment viable. Various ways have been explored to bring in foreign capital and expertise via joint ventures. The first stage in Western involvement in the telecommunications sector was the setting up of cellular networks and joint ventures to provide new exchanges. But Hungary is a small market – probably too small to meet most operators' revenue expectations.

The government prevaricated on the proposals for the privatisation of MATAV (the Hungarian telecommunications company operating under the aegis of the Ministry of Transport, Communications and Water Management) because of its reluctance to address crucial questions. In November 1992, the Hungarian parliament after a year of controversy finally approved a law on telecommunications, under which foreign operators in Hungary will be able to compete for local networks, mobile communications and data transmission contracts. This transforms MATAV into the holder of a 25-year concession to operate the country's local line network. But in the 56 regions, competing bids may be entered to win concessions and provide local services. The fragmented structure that seems the likely result of the Telecommunications Act may create serious disincentives to investment. Populist pressures will probably keep prices low, but will not generate the cash flow that would make the investment attractive to foreign interests.

Mobile phones

Hungary has awarded its two national digital telephone licences. Penetration of analogue mobile phones has been quicker than in the West. It has been reported that half the subscribers to these services do not have access to a standard telephone line. Westel, a mobile phone joint venture involving US West and MATAV, and another consortium of national telecoms companies from the Netherlands, Sweden and Finland, have paid more than US$100 million between them for the two licences.

Very small aperture terminal (VSAT)

To overcome the problems linked with a poor telephone network, some companies, in particular AB, have decided to experiment with VSAT and install a network of small satellite dishes. A US$75,000 feasibility study is under way in Hungary for the installation of a shared-hub multi-client VSAT service with an estimated capacity of 2000 sites. Hungary could become a pioneer in the integration of computers and telecommunications because there is no resistance from national telecommunications operators to the spread of this technology as in other European countries.

Part III

The Options for Western Business

21

Import and Export

KPMG Peat Marwick

Hungary is a trading nation. Half of its GDP is derived from exports – twice the average for OECD nations. Trade liberalisation since 1988 has led to a massive increase in the number of companies involved in import and export activities. In 1991 there were 33,000 such companies. In 1993, this number had more than doubled to 71,000. Under foreign trade regulations, foreign trade activities can be pursued by all companies possessing the appropriate expertise. The only requirement is to register at the National Bank of Hungary. There has also been a fundamental shift in the geographical export and import patterns.

A NEW FRAMEWORK FOR INTERNATIONAL TRADE

A so-called Europe Agreement was signed between the EC and Hungary in December 1991. Pending ratification by member states, Interim Agreements implementing the trade chapters of the agreement came into effect in March 1992. They commit the signatories to free trade within 10 years with the EC dismantling its barriers faster, in 5 years. It is too early to judge the overall impact that the Europe Agreement will have.

Hungary also signed a mutual trade agreement with Czechoslovakia (now the Czech and Slovak Republics) and Poland on 21 December 1992. This has significantly reduced customs barriers between the four countries. Duties on up to 30 per cent of industrial goods were to be eliminated completely from March 1993 onwards, with the rest to be phased out over 8 years.

Towards the end of January 1993, representatives of Hungary also initialled a series of multilateral articles of a free trade agreement with EFTA. These are similar to the Europe Agreement in that it provides for immediate free access for most industrial goods and a 10-year timetable in the case of sensitive products. As with the EC Agreement, they exclude agricultural products. It is estimated that this will mean 85 per cent of industrial exports (worth US$1.3 billion in 1992) will have free access to EFTA markets. The EFTA agreement is accompanied by bilateral agreements covering agriculture (the most difficult issue had been the exports of agricultural products to Austria).

IMPORTING INTO HUNGARY

Licensing requirements have been gradually eliminated. Now 90 per cent of Hungarian industrial production is exposed to licence- and quota-free import competition. This includes the whole of the machine industry, a part of light industry and most agricultural products. These products may be imported freely (only a notification obligation has to be fulfilled) and the value of the imports is to be paid in forints to the bank in exchange for foreign currency. Services that may be imported freely include trade marks, patents and copyrights, technical information, software consultancy and marketing consultancy. The 10 per cent of goods not on the liberalised list include:

- household chemicals;
- footwear;
- precious metals;
- vehicles;
- chemical compounds;
- telecommunications equipment; and
- some agricultural products such as meat and cheeses.

Some goods, particularly agricultural products, are subject to a quota system.

The Ministry of Foreign Economic Relations announces quotas every six months. The importer must apply as soon as the new values and volume for a particular product are announced but cannot ask for more than 5–10 per cent of the quota depending on the product. It should be noted tht quotas will disappear due to the Association Agreement with the EC and that often the volume of products imported in some categories was less than the quotas set, due to a lesser demand caused by recession.

Most business is done on a straightforward commercial basis. Countertrade, switch deals and compensation deals do take place but only to a limited extent. These must in any case take into account existing import licensing and quota arrangements in force in the exporter's country.

Customs

A new Customs Act is under consideration in an effort to bring Hungarian customs legislation into line with that of its major trading partners. Customs duties are administered by the Customs Administration of the Ministry of Finance. The key points about the new legislation are as follows:

- dutiable values are in line with GATT;

- there are detailed rules of origin; and

- the availability of temporary import status is severely restricted.

Imports are subject to customs duties. Hungary uses the Customs Co-operation Council Nomenclature classification and accords the UK most favoured nation status. Documentation and payment of duties is usually arranged by the importer in Hungary. Generally, an invoice/delivery note is sufficient unless the nature of the goods requires otherwise. Imports are usually made on an FOB or CIF basis. The importer must deposit the hard currency equivalent of the cost of the proposed imports and, if required, the import licence issued by the Ministry of International Economic Relations.

Duties

Customs procedures are regulated by the joint decree of the Ministry of Finance and the Ministry for Foreign Trade. The majority of imports are taxed at the 10–25 per cent rate of duty. Foreign investors may import goods temporarily without paying duties if they provide adequate security for goods. The goods subject to relief may be kept for a maximum of 12 months but this may be extended upon request.

Capital assets which form part of a foreign shareholder's

contribution to the capital may be imported duty-free, although VAT has to be paid as of 1 January 1993. The company is required to hold the assets for at least three years. If the assets are sold or rented before the end of the three years, the customs duty and VAT have to be paid together with a penalty for late payment. Exemption from paying customs duty does not eliminate the requirement to pay customs clearance charges (2 per cent) and statistical dues (3 per cent) which must be paid whenever anything is imported.

Imports are cleared on the day of entry and customs duties are payable within 14 days. Where applicable, VAT and excise are levied and must be paid within 15 days. The rates are the same as for domestic supplies. The VAT base includes customs duties. VAT is determined by the Customs Administration at the same time as it assesses the customs duties payable.

Goods can be imported by road, rail, river or through Budapest airport. There are onward transport facilities. There are free port facilities in Budapest and provision for loading and unloading of barges and small vessels. Transit warehouses are also available.

Customs-free zones

Companies with foreign shareholders may be set up in customs-free zones for two purposes: industrial production or for commercial warehousing and ancillary activities.

A customs-free zone is extra-territorial from the point of view of customs, foreign exchange and foreign trade regulations. Companies doing business in a customs-free zone are treated as foreign companies. Goods brought into Hungary from a customs-free zone count as imports and goods brought into the zone count as exports. A company in a customs-free zone may raise credit abroad and pursue foreign trade activities without restriction.

Getting paid

Hungary does not have a fully convertible currency. Despite the level of debt, Hungarian companies do usually have a fair payment history, although delays are quite common. Tried and tested methods of payment such as letters of credit and cash in advance are the most commonplace. If credit is sought, a letter of credit, guaranteed by a reputable bank, is advisable. Confirmed letters of credit are not as essential in Hungary as they are in other parts of the region. ECGD cover is available for Hungary. If the buyer's credit history is patchy or non-existent, tread with extreme caution.

Distribution

In the past, foreign trade organizations were the only point of contact for all import/export operations and enjoyed a monopoly position on whole sectors. Now, in the process of being privatised, they lack focus but they are probably worth visiting once to ascertain market conditions.

The whole distribution chain for consumer goods has changed at a remarkable speed. The most important wholesalers are usually former state owned companies and are in the process of privatisation.

EXPORTING FROM HUNGARY

Quantitative restrictions on Hungarian exports

In addition to the membership of free trade areas mentioned above, Hungary has been granted most favoured nation status by a number of its trading partners, including Austria, Australia, Canada, Japan and the USA. This gives Hungary a tariff treatment equal to the lowest rate offered to other countries.

However, check for quota and other quantitative restrictions on Hungarian imports into other countries. More than 58 per cent of Hungary's exports to the EC fall into the category deemed sensitive – ie agriculture, processed foods, textiles, chemicals and steel. These remain subject to severe protectionist measures and are liable to face barriers over and above the usual tariff. The EC has fixed anti-dumping duties of up to 21.7 per cent on steel tubes after complaints from EC producers that Hungarian imports, among others, were undermining the industry. However, if steel producers give price undertakings, they will be exempt from the duties.

A temporary ban on meat-based and dairy products from Central and Eastern Europe in response to an outbreak of foot and mouth disease in Croatia irritated the Hungarian authorities because of the blanket nature of the ban. The ban was quickly lifted after the authorities agreed to quarantine periods.

Barter operations with the CIS grew between 1989 and 1992 as a means to circumvent increasing trading and payment difficulties. However these have proved less and less popular with Huangarian exporters because it is not possible to construct stable networks with CIS importers for countertrade operations.

Specifications

Many Western companies have been regular takers of Hungarian goods under licensing, contract manufacturing and other arrangements. Hungary is in the process of implementing EC and international technical standards to products made in the country. Write precise quality specifications into your contract as well as delivery times, and never agree to accept goods from a Hungarian supplier without making sure he can meet your quality requirements.

Foreign currency earnings and export credit

Companies may not generally retain the foreign currency they earn from exports. Foreign currency is received through a licensed bank and converted into forints. This does create exchange risks as the forint was substantially devalued in 1993.

Export credit

There is a new export credit institution in Hungary which provides exporters with guarantees against political and country risk and provides export credit and financing facilities.

22

Trade Finance

Creditanstalt-Bank Verien

A CHANGED MARKET

The transformation of the Hungarian economy from a centrally planned into a market oriented one – a process which started as early as in the mid-1980s – obviously has had an enormous impact on trade finance as it has on other financial markets.

Focusing on trade finance, the changes can be summarised as follows:

1. Previously, all import letters of credit on behalf of Hungarian importers were issued by the National Bank of Hungary or by the Hungarian Foreign Trade Bank. The National Bank of Hungary has now been transformed into a central bank and has ceased all commercial transactions. The role of the National Bank in exercising commercial banking functions and handling Hungarian foreign trade was taken over by the newly founded commercial banks.

2. Hungarian imports had – according to local regulation – to be handled by letters of credit if a single transaction exceeded a certain amount. This regulation has been recently withdrawn, offering Hungarian importers the freedom to negotiate payment conditions with their suppliers as is usual in any developed economy, and reducing the volume of import letters of credit substantially.

3. The number of potential importers in Hungary has

increased due to the liberalisation of the economy. The foreign trade organisations have lost their monopoly. Every company is now entitled to carry out foreign trade transactions without permission, and the foreign trade organisations must compete with them. Due to deterioration of the economy, imports have been reduced quite substantially (down 5 per cent in the first quarter of 1993 compared to the first quarter of 1992). The reduced volume of imports is handled by an increased number of banks.

4. The risk of both importers and banks in Hungary has increased. Importers are either relatively new companies without a track-record, or are long-established companies burdened with the past. The banks, except those with a foreign shareholding, are also either new or have to bear the non-performing loans from the days of the old regime. In addition, bank staff are not trained as in Western countries and to a great extent have only limited experience even in 'standard' banking products such as foreign payments, guarantee business and letters of credit.

5. The forint has acquired internal convertibility – ie for import transactions foreign exchange approval is no longer needed. In fact, an importer can obtain the necessary foreign currency through his bank.

An increasing number of transactions are effected on an 'open account' basis. The banks are no longer involved as collecting agents as in the case of 'cash against documents' or as obligor, such as in letter of credit business, but only transfer the amounts involved. This development obviously leads to inexpensive money transfers but ignores the credit risks involved.

In paying upon receipt of invoice (regardless of payment at sight of deferred terms) the Hungarian importer avoids the cost of having the letter of credit opened by the bank and the cash collateral payment which he often has to provide to his bankers. The exporter avoids the advising and (as the case may be) the confirming costs for the letter of credit by taking the payment risk himself.

Apparently a high percentage of Western exporters are prepared to take this risk. Also some export agencies and/or private risk insurers will consider taking such risks provided they arise from a long-standing relationship.

FINANCING TECHNIQUES

It is worth mentioning that instruments securing payment obligations in ongoing business relationships, such as letters of guarantee or standby letters of credit, are quite uncommon in Hungary. Bills of exchange and/or promissory notes to secure payment – whether guaranteed by a bank or not – are almost unknown in Hungary. The financing of imports is either carried out by local banks (forint liquidity is relatively high) or on deferred payment terms by the exporter. As the volume of trade finance transactions is decreasing and because the country risk is nowadays acceptable for short-term transactions, for most banks in Western Europe the margins for trade finance transactions are on a downward trend.

Today the standard foreign trade-related business in Hungary can be categorised into three types of transaction:

- Letters of credit, payable at sight or on deferred terms of up to 360 days.

- Loans granted to Hungarian banks, drawable against sight letters of credit for the exporter. The respective letter of credit looks like a sight l/c, but the issuing bank draws in reimbursement for its obligation under a loan granted by the advising bank. As some Hungarian banks can already refinance themselves to some extent on the international money market, the loan business as mentioned above is decreasing.

- Pre-export financing facilities are sometimes required by Hungarian companies. The big task for the Hungarian banks with regard to trade finance is the development of mechanisms to finance Hungarian exports. This includes the foundation of an export agency similar to institutions already operating in Western Europe. First steps in this direction have already been taken.

Assuming a steady improvement in the Hungarian economy, in the long run trade finance for exports to Hungary will follow the West European pattern. One of the key issues will be the assessment of Hungarian corporate credit standing, and then being in a position to carry direct company risk. The joint venture companies are important in this connection.

To secure payments in newly established relationships, bank guarantees or letters of credit will remain the main instruments (combined with forfeiting the respective payment terms).

23

Agencies, Distributorships and Franchising

SJ Berwin & Co

When seeking to trade or sell goods or services in another country, the manufacturer, supplier or owner of the relevant rights often prefers to do so at a distance, rather than involving himself directly in the conduct of business in that country. This means finding someone willing and able to take on the role of representing, promoting, selling, delivering and protecting the goods, services, name, style or system in that country. This normally leads to the appointment of an agent or distributor. On the other hand, certain types of situations involving the use of a name, intellectual property rights or know-how may necessitate the grant of a licence, and in other special situations a franchise may be more appropriate. In this chapter we shall consider three of these arrangements – agency, distribution and franchise (licences are examined in Chapter 25).

The appointment of an agent or representative involves the giving of certain authority to a local person to act on behalf of the foreign party in the particular country. Generally, an agent has little or no authority to bind or commit the foreign principal except to a certain limited extent. An agent holds no goods and provides no services itself; this is all done by the principal. A distributor, on the other hand, represents itself, selling the goods or providing the services of the foreign partner in its own name and for its own account. The distributor generally holds a stock of the goods in question, which it buys from the foreign manufacturer or supplier and sells on to the customer.

A franchise is a mixture of a licence arrangement and a distribution contract. Generally it involves the use of a well-known name and system for marketing and producing the goods or services in question. By using the name of the franchisor (the person giving the franchise) there is a ready market for a widely known name. As the system of marketing and, in particular, production, are well known and tested, the customer expects (as does the franchisor) that a certain standard found in all franchisees of the particular name or product will be maintained.

LEGAL REGULATIONS

Few countries have mandatory rules relating to agency, distribution and franchise arrangements, and in many cases there are few laws to regulate the contractual situation. Hungarian law is not vastly different, in that while the Civil Code contains express rules on commercial agency, there are no laws to regulate distributorship and franchise arrangements. Accordingly, as with most contracts in Hungary, there is a wide freedom for the parties to agree their own terms. Except for agency, because there are no dispositive rules on which to fall back if the parties' agreement is silent, parties should specify as fully as possible their respective rights, duties, commitments and undertakings under contracts of this type. (Also, it should be remembered that where a resident Hungarian national is appointed as a foreign company's agent a written foreign trade contract must be entered into between the parties).

Terms of appointment

In all cases the terms and conditions agreed by the parties reflect the essence of the arrangement. Though they may not vary greatly from other countries, there are certain essential terms which should be sought when entering into agency, distribution and franchise agreements in Hungary. This chapter aims to provide a checklist of essential and relevant terms for consideration in each case.

AGENCY

A Decree of the Presidential Council (No. 8 of 1978), still in force, deals with the rights and duties of commercial agents with particular reference to foreign trade contracts, and the obligation to provide after-sales services unless otherwise agreed. This law was intended specifically for Hungarian entities or individuals appointed agents in Hungary for foreign manufacturers or suppliers of goods and services. The rules are applicable notwithstanding the changed economic system in Hungary.

Obligations of commercial agents

The law states the obligations of the agent include:

- the right to conclude a foreign trade contract on behalf of the foreign principal, subject to the authority or instructions given by the principal;

- taking all customary and expected measures to promote sales of goods, services and rights of the principal;

- informing the principal of changes in market conditions which may be important for the principal's business strategy;

- exercising great care in selecting customers for the principal;

- allowing the principal access to the books and records of the agency;

- making offers and concluding contracts on the terms and instructions of the principal;

- not to inform third parties or to use information acquired during the course of the agency;

- immediately to inform the principal if he obtains knowledge of a violation of the rights of the principal; and

- not to represent a competitor of the principal nor to compete with the principal on his own account.

Remuneration

Agents are entitled to remuneration and this is normally in the form of commissions based on the value of contracts concluded under the agency agreement. However, there is no reason why an agent should not be paid a fixed sum rather than a commission. The law is silent on the amount of commission and this is a matter for agreement between the parties. Commissions are also payable on contracts concluded before termination of the agency even though the contract is only performed after termination.

Termination

Agency is presumed to terminate when the duration period specified has elapsed. However, if the appointment is for an indefinite duration it may only be terminated on three months notice, effective at the end of a calendar year. The law makes no provision for compensation on the termination of an agency, but this possibility can also be expressly excluded in the contract to ensure there is no uncertainty.

After-sales arrangements

Where there is an obligation to provide after-sales servicing (whether under a guarantee or otherwise) the agent is required to do this at his own cost, although the principal is bound to compensate the agent. The scope of these after-sales services is generally covered in the after-sales service agreement. This involves the agent maintaining a stock of spare parts and a repair shop with suitably trained staff to carry out repairs. The principal is required to supply the agent with information, technical instructions and the spare parts to enable him to provide the after-sales service.

Agency contract checklist

The essential terms to be covered in an agency agreement include the following:

- the subject matter of the agency – ie, specific goods and services;
- the territory of the agency, including the right to promote and conclude sale arrangements outside the territory;
- the specific authority of the agent to bind and commit the principal;
- the obligation of the principal to supply, or the agent to purchase, samples, promotional and advertising materials for the products;
- the agent not to represent competitive products;

- the agent to keep secret all confidential information relating to the principal's business or the goods or services in question;

- the terms of payment, including in respect of contracts concluded but not performed and part performance;

- commission rates, fixed payments and repayment of expenses;

- duration and the grounds for termination of the agency, and the notice to be given of termination;

- obligation to forward payments received for the principal immediately; and

- warranty and repair undertakings for goods being sold by the agent and the after-sales services to be provided by the principal and agent.

DISTRIBUTORSHIP

As already noted, there are no legal rules specifically concerned with distributorship arrangements. Accordingly, relying on the basic contract rules and freedom of contract, it is for the parties to determine the form, extent and terms and conditions of their distributorship arrangement. The dispositive provisions of the Civil Code will apply to the contract itself, so the parties should be as clear as possible as regards their respective rights and obligations.

Essential characteristics of a distribution agreement

Before finalising a distribution agreement in Hungary, it should be clear specifically what the manufacturer or supplier is seeking in Hungary.

1. Is the intention to develop the market in Hungary only, or is the Hungarian distributor a base for Central and Eastern Europe generally?

2. Is there already a market for the goods or services in Hungary or is the intention to develop a new market? This may be relevant in respect of support for the distributor

and the level of sales for the fixing of minimum purchase obligations.

3. Are the goods and services sold or provided under a trade mark or name? If so, such trade mark or name must be registered to ensure protection.

4. If an after-sales maintenance and repairs service is to be provided, has the distributor the necessary infrastructure, skill, expertise and technical knowledge? If not, will the manufacturer or supplier provide the training, manpower and support for this purpose?

5. Are the goods and services appropriate for the Hungarian market or will adaptations be necessary (eg to comply with local electrical standards)? If so, whose responsibility will these be?

6. If there are any import restrictions for the goods to be distributed, who will be responsible for obtaining the necessary import licences?

Major obligations of the distributor

If the distribution arrangement is to be successful it is essential that the distributor be required to perform certain duties:

- to promote the sale and distribution of the goods and services in the territory;

- to purchase from the manufacturer/supplier a minimum quantity of goods and to resell a minimum quantity in the territory;

- to pay the manufacturer/supplier in hard, convertible currency for the goods;

- to hold a stock of goods, spare parts and accessories as appropriate; and

- to keep the manufacturer/supplier informed of market conditions, any competing products and any counterfeit products, plus any other infringement of patents, trade marks and other rights of the manufacturer/supplier.

Areas of concern

Due to the particular nature of the Hungarian market, certain issues will need careful consideration:

- Who is to be liable for damage incurred by users of the goods or third parties due to defects in the goods? Relevant here is Hungary's law on Product Liability (Act X of 1993), which is similar to the model adopted by the Council of Europe.

- Environmental concerns are of major and increasing importance. While it may be possible at present to sell goods that are not environmentally friendly, this may be short term because Hungary will be implementing strict environmental controls in the next few years.

- The pricing of the goods for the Hungarian market-place should reflect the problems in Hungary. However, discriminatory pricing or selling at a loss, even in the short term and to secure a market position, can have detrimental results in the long term.

Other matters which will need to be settled include the duration of the distribution agreement, the conditions on which the agreement may be terminated, the obligation on the manufacturer to repurchase unsold stock after termination of the agreement, the purchase price of the goods and the terms for delivery, the law to govern the agreement and the system and venue for dispute settlement.

FRANCHISING

There is no Hungarian law on franchising. Accordingly, subject to the law on the protection of intellectual property rights, the parties are free to and should set out as fully as possible the specific terms and conditions of their agreement. Many of the principles and concerns discussed in connection with agency, distribution and licence agreements are also relevant to franchise agreements.

A franchisor looking to grant a franchise in Hungary must decide on the following:

- Does it wish to repatriate profits in the short term? This may be difficult in the absence of a fully convertible currency.

- The possibility of developing the franchise within Hungary and having a whole series of outlets.

- Whether to retain a share of the franchise business as a joint venture partner.

- Whether to assist with the financing of the franchise either through direct lending, credit or raw materials purchase.

Another major issue in a franchise arrangement is the need to establish and maintain the basic standard of production, presentation and quality. This can be dealt with generally through skill seconded to the franchisee and requiring the franchisee to purchase raw materials from the franchisor or its nominated suppliers, and by providing training and supervision. However, the infrastructure necessary to maintain standards may not be available at the present time.

Financing for an independent Hungarian franchisee will present various difficulties in the light of the difficulty of determining value and taking security on land and other property.

24

Marketing

Saatchi & Saatchi Advertising Worldwide

The first four years after the fall of communism have been characterised by a sort of 'gold rush' mood. A myriad of new companies have been set up, and 'joint venture' were magic words in Hungarian business life. After the initial euphoria faded a more realistic perspective took over. Now, at the end of 1993, most major multinational companies had serious difficulties in forecasting business and setting up proper budgets. Growth of up to 300 per cent per annum has been the rule rather than the exception, and 1994 will be the first year when market shares become stablised and companies can seriously start to consolidate their business. Certain industries are very competitive already, like the coffee market and the car market.

Since the political changes, a new generation of brand managers and marketing directors has come up through the ranks, or been flown in from abroad. Notably, the latter group does not, generally, appreciate the hardship of the early pioneering days when improvisation and good instincts were more important than sound marketing know-how. This new generation of marketing people – especially those who have come to Hungary recently – demand and expect to receive Western standards. They are sometimes unaware that only minor gains have been made in the field of telecommunications; that suppliers only have three years experience; etc. It is therefore up to the service industries to make strenuous efforts to maintain pressure for the level of service required in a competitive environment. This naturally brings higher costs.

Companies are compelled to fly in experienced professionals from abroad with at least two objectives – training young,

Hungarian successors and servicing clients at the level of Western standards.

PRODUCT REPRESENTATION

It is estimated that roughly 75 per cent of all major Western products and brands have now been launched in the Hungarian market. (Saatchi & Saatchi Budapest launched 24 products within 14 months between October 1991 and November 1992.) In tandem with the decrease in the number of new product launches, the role of advertising has also changed. Whereas through 1992 advertising was considered to be more important as a source of information (informing consumers about new products available for the first time in the Hungarian market), advertising is now becoming more of a marketing tool, like in any other sophisticated Western market. Now, advertising is about positioning brands, distinguishing them from similar competitive products and teasing/encouraging consumers to choose brand 'x' over brand 'y', although price still plays an important role for the consumer in Hungary.

In the field of research there have also been some marked improvements over the past four years. There are now several (international and local) market research companies operating in Hungary, the majority of them providing accurate and reliable data. Both quantitative and qualitative (focus group) research studies can be undertaken with reliable results, the added advantage being that this can be achieved at a considerable saving in budgetary terms. The facilities offered by most good research companies include viewing facilities and/or taped evidence, with a summary document in two (or more) languages if required.

Media monitoring companies are slowly catching up to the demands of the more sophisticated agencies, so media planners can now be made accountable for their plans.

MEDIA

Print

Hungary continues to increase the amount of publications produced (at present there are over 2000). Because of this there is very little loyalty from readers who are constantly being enticed to purchase other titles. Readership is an average 40/60 per cent Budapest/rural split. The consequence of saturation of print media is the increasing development of niche titles (some of dubious quality). New titles often have a high mortality rate causing advertising agencies to be cautious.

Hungarians like to read daily newspapers as shown by the 13 national dailies and the 40 regional dailies currently available. Around 79 per cent of all adults read a daily newspaper at least once in 7 days. Curiously, morning readership of the dailies is minimal.

The proliferation of titles has meant that pricing has risen constantly as the quality titles have been 'corralled' by the larger publishing houses, giving the giants a virtual monopoly as a result. At the risk of over-generalising, it can be said that 1993 saw the better titles improving. In contrast to previous years there has been a strong move towards Western printing standards with paper and reprographic quality increasing substantially. This has drawn Western advertisers towards this medium and, as a result, this sector has seen its market share increase.

At present Hungary is in the unfortunate situation where demand exceeds supply in the choice of titles as there are still relatively few quality publications. The results are spiralling prices and incredibly long lead times affecting many campaigns. Inflation on media in magazines is currently at 50 per cent. This rate is not expected to decrease year-on-year.

Television

Currently there are 8,226,000 TV sets in Hungary watched by 99 per cent of Hungarians aged 14 years of age and over. This medium has the highest coverage and reach into households.

Around 91 per cent of all adults watch television every day. This is a staggering figure and hence television commands the lion's share of advertising expenditure in Hungary; estimated to be 42 per cent for 1993. This figure has increased dramatically since 1989 (10 per cent) due to improved programming strategies and better programmes. Numerous Western programmes such as *Kojak*, etc can now be seen on Hungarian television.

Two channels are available – Magyar TV1 and TV2. TV1 has the higher audience levels and accrues approximately 65 per cent of the viewing. Unification of the two channels in September 1992 meant that programming began to derive from a single source. A third commercial station has been proposed for 1994, but this has yet to be confirmed. TV in Hungary on a cost per thousand basis is relatively cheap compared to its Western counterparts.

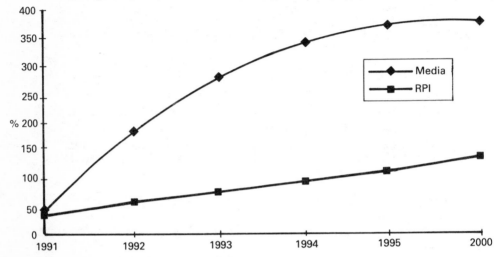

Figure 24.1   *Media inflation vs the RPI, 1991–2000*

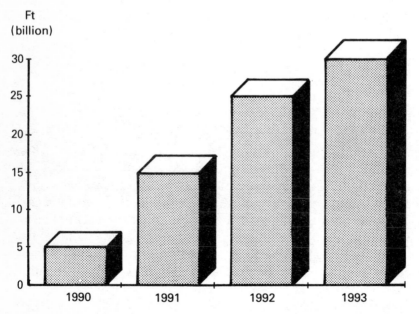

Figure 24.2   *Media expenditure year-on-year, 1990–93*

Radio

Currently there are six radio stations available, three of which are privately owned. This medium can generally be regarded as set to improve in quality rapidly, mainly due to impetus from the three private stations. Altogether, they have a potential daily reach of 73 per cent, an improvement of 1 per cent on the 1992 figure. This is predominantly a morning medium with peak listenership taking place in the first part of the day. There is a limited ability to receive new radio stations as the frequencies are only available on new radios. At present this is the most cost effective of all the media. It is expected to take 5 per cent of all advertising expenditure in 1993.

Recently, 40 licences have been offered by the state and numerous tenders have been submitted. So far, no licences have been awarded.

Outdoor

Outdoor advertising has grown tremendously with the current availability of over 10,000 sites across Hungary. This was due mainly to the tobacco companies.

The most common size is the 24-sheet, which accounts for 24 per cent of all sites in Budapest. Predominantly a rural medium, 600 sites make up a solid national campaign. Due to the vast amount of sites this is classified as a negotiable medium and suppliers are willing to offer specific sites, times and creative changes. Despite this, posters are still a relatively expensive medium.

Hungary is very well developed with over 10 stationary site contractors and the ability to utilise mobile billboards as well. Budapest has seen the development of stationary building sites, mostly neon, which can be seen on the skyline. A large proportion are electronic, and well-positioned in areas of high automobile and pedestrian traffic.

FUTURE TRENDS

As can be seen from Figure 24.1, we can expect a decrease in inflation in all media. The year 1993 sees the increase at 100 per cent on average across all media, but the estimated long-term decline will bring this figure to more like 40 per cent by the end of 1994, early 1995. Currently, it stands, in real terms, at 75 per cent.

Advertising expenditure in 1993 is expected to hit an all-time high of Ft30 billion (US$400 million), which represents an increase of approx 25 per cent year-on-year. At present there is no sign of this rate of increase slowing.

25

Licensing

SJ Berwin & Co

INTELLECTUAL PROPERTY RIGHTS

Intellectual property is the term used for various intangible forms of valuable rights that have no physical form. They include copyright, patents, trade marks, trade names, service marks, industrial designs and secret know-how. These rights, due to their very nature, are only valuable because of the possibility of one party being able to retain ownership and exclusive use of them in a particular territory. In some cases ownership of these rights can be proved by registration or a certificate of first use; in other cases it is necessary to prove proprietary right acquired by exclusive use.

In every country the rights attaching to such intellectual property vary according to the local law and the country's international commitments. Hungary has well-developed intellectual property laws, in particular on patents (Act II of 1969, as amended by Decree Law 5 of 1983 and Decree Laws 77 of 1989 and 78 of 1989), trade marks (Act IX of 1969), industrial designs (Decree Law 28 of 1978) and copyright (Act III of 1969, as amended by Decree Law 27 of 1978). These laws are supported by Hungary being party to the major international conventions dealing with industrial property rights including:

- Convention establishing the World Intellectual Property Organisation (WIPO);

- Paris Convention for the Protection of Industrial Property;

- Madrid Agreement for the Repression of False or Deceptive Indications of Source on Goods;

- Hague Agreement Concerning the International Deposit of Industrial Design;

- Nice Agreement Concerning the International Classification of Goods and Services for the Purposes of the Registration of Marks;

- Lisbon Agreement for the Protection of Appellations of Origin and their International Registration;

- Locarno Agreement Establishing an International Classification for Industrial Designs;

- the Patent Co-operation Treaty; and

- the International Convention for the Protection of New Varieties of Plant (UPOV).

LICENSING

As intellectual property rights give exclusive or monopoly right of use to the registered owner, the only way another party can use the rights is with the permission of the owner – ie, by a licence. Licences provide a means for the licensee to obtain the right to use intellectual property rights; for the licensor it is generally an additional source of revenue as a payment for use of the right. A patent or industrial design licence avoids the time, delay and cost of research and development on the part of the licensee. 'Buying' the technology rights or know-how from the owner enables the licensee, in theory at least, to reach the same technological standard as the licensor and to try and develop its technology from that stage. Copyright and trade mark licences, in their own way, give a source of immediate additional income to the licensor, through a new product or a 'cachet' that assists in the sale of products which carry that mark.

Before granting licences into a particular territory, the licensor will need to determine the protection for his intellectual property rights in that country. This depends, as already noted, on the law and that country's membership of certain international treaty arrangements. This is also, in some respects, true when taking a licence from a person claiming to be the owner of particular rights.

Essential legal issues for licensors in Hungary

It will be useful then, before considering the main characteristics of the different types of licence, to review briefly the legal rules in Hungary. Questions of particular concern include:

- Is the licensor/licensee authorised to give the undertakings that are contained in the licence? In particular does the licensor own the particular rights?

- Are the Hungarian rights genuinely protected and not owned by some other person in the licensed territory?

- Is the licensee in Hungary also the person who will exploit the rights in that territory?

- Are confidentiality undertakings and obligations enforceable?

- How can monopoly rights be protected if infringed and how can counterfeiting be stopped?

Registration of industrial property rights

The National Office of Inventions is the central regulatory body responsible for the registration of all industrial property rights (except copyright), whether of domestic or foreign origin, and for the preparation of legislation for parliament in the field of industrial property.

PATENTS

The subject matter for registration as a patent is something which is 'new, represents progress, is of a technical nature and is capable of practical application'. This generally includes industrial, electrical, mechanical and other engineering processes, the manufacturing processes for the creation of all kinds of products, including chemicals, medicines, foods for human and animal consumption and new plant and animal breeds.

The first to apply for the patent has priority to exploit it. Any invention which is made in the course of employment (ie, where the employee has the obligation to develop inventions in a particular field) will be the property of the employer. But the inventor still retains certain rights in respect of royalties, even if the right to use the invention and to grant licences belongs to the employer. The patent is provisionally protected from the moment of application and, provided it is registered, remains valid for 20 years from the date of application. The rights conferred by registration are simply to manufacture, use and market the product produced using the patent.

Where a patent is infringed in Hungary, the foreign patent owner can seek the following remedies:

- a declaration that the patent has been infringed;

- an injunction to prohibit abuse of the patent;

- an order for a payment to the patent owner of an amount equivalent to the amount by which the infringer has been enriched by abusing the patent;

- an order for seizure of all products manufactured infringing the patent and of any instruments used for so doing; and

- an order for full compensation.

These issues are decided at first instance by the National Office of Inventions, but parties may appeal to the Metropolitan Court in Budapest.

An important consideration in Hungary is that if the patent is not exploited in Hungary within four years of the application or three years from the date of the grant of the patent, a compulsory licence may be granted to any party who applies to work the patent in Hungary. This rule, which was intended to ensure that practical and advanced processes were utilised, is likely to be abolished in the future.

INDUSTRIAL DESIGNS

The external shape of an industrial product ('design') may be entitled to registration if:

- it is new;

- it is not detrimental to the normal use of the product;

- it is not merely the consequence of the technical solution or the purpose of the product;

- its purpose is not identical to that of a design enjoying

earlier priority or is not similar to another design so as to create a risk of confusion.

The design shall be entitled to protection from the date the design is registered by the National Office of Inventions, with retroactive effect to the date of application. The protection is granted for a term of five years but, at the request of the owner, it may be renewed for an additional five years.

The scope of design protection is determined by the external shape being identified by means of a photograph or a graphical representation deposited in the Design Register.

Subject to reciprocity, design protection shall not extend to means of movement and transport in transit, nor to merchandise of foreign origin not intended for sale in Hungary.

TRADE MARKS AND SERVICE MARKS

Trade and service marks are used to distinguish goods and services of a particular source, from goods and services from another source, and are registrable where such goods and services are of a special or different character. A trade or service mark may be granted over any form of pictorial device, image, words, audio or visual signal.

A mark is provisionally protected for 10 years from the date of application for registration. The grant of a trade mark may be excluded where:

- it is likely to create confusion;
- it infringes the rights of third parties;
- it is identical or confusingly similar to a trade or service mark held by another party which is well known in Hungary, even if that mark is not registered in Hungary;
- it consists of the flag or pictorial device of any state, authority or international organisation.

COPYRIGHT

Copyright protects original literary, scientific and artistic creations and generally vests in the author of the work. The copyright owner is free to control the way in which, and the time at which, the work is made available to the public and is entitled to remuneration for the use of the author's work at any time. These rights cannot be transferred but may be passed on at death.

A work which has been published outside Hungary first, is covered by copying the protection in Hungary if the author is a Hungarian citizen, or if the author is entitled to protection under an international convention or on the basis of reciprocity.

A copyright owner can apply to the court for the same remedies that are open to patent and trade mark owners.

KNOW-HOW

Know-how is, in principle, protected by Section 86(4) of the Civil Code, which reads 'persons are entitled to protection of economic, technical and organisational knowledge and experience having financial value'.

Know-how is difficult to define and even more difficult to regulate. It is not in itself subject to registration. It gives a monopoly right to the owner because he has developed and kept it secret or confidential. There are no rules dealing with the licensing of know-how to Hungarian entities. The way in which this information is passed on depends therefore, primarily, on the terms of the licence agreement between the Western partner and the Hungarian party.

OTHER ISSUES

Contracting partners

As the law contains no express rules on licensing of intellectual property rights, the detail of any licensing agreement is a matter for the parties and therefore falls subject to the provisions of the Civil Code covering contracts. All legal entities are able to enter into such contracts. It should be remembered that it is the first party entered on the register that holds the ownership of the industrial property right in the area of patents and trade marks. With reference to copyrights, it is the author who holds the rights. Therefore a licence can only stem from an agreement with that party.

Essential licence considerations

Every licence agreement should take account of the particular interests of the licensor and licensee, the subject-matter of the licence and the legal problems and uncertainties in the territory in which the licence is granted. As Hungarian law contains no regulatory framework for licence agreements, parties should specify to the fullest extent possible their respective rights and obligations and the effects of particular problems or occurrences.

A foreign owner of intellectual property rights granting a licence to a Hungarian licensor should consider the following issues:

- The territory in which the licence is effective. Can the licensee, for example, sell products manufactured under a patent licence or carrying the trade mark outside Hungary, into either Western Europe or the former Comecon territories?

- Restrictions on the use of the intellectual property rights.

- Duration and conditions for termination of the licence.

- The licence fee or royalty. This could be a fixed sum or a per item royalty according to the nature of the licence. In this context the foreign licensor will be concerned at the withholding tax applied to royalties.

- The obligation to pay the licence fee or royalty in hard currency, or taking some goods made under the licence as a part payment.

- The obligation on the licensor to give a licence on updated or developed technology, patents or designs to the licensee, or the right to other intellectual property of the licensor.

- Whether the licensee must transfer to the licensor all developments and alterations made to the patent or know-how, and assist this being registered in the licensor's name. An alternative is the obligation to license back such developments on advantageous or pre-agreed terms.

- Improvements to the original design of the product and alterations to the end-product.

- Marking products and the restrictions on use of trade marks and service marks by the licence-holder.

- Performance requirements and specifications on the end-product.

- Restrictions on the sub-licensing of any work by the holder of the licence.

- The way in which accounting for the products and sales will be conducted between the parties.

- The requirements of confidentiality on the licensee.

26

Project Finance

Creditanstalt-Bankverein

There are three important economic developments currently under way in Hungary that are expected to drive the country's economic and social development in the future: the privatisation programme, direct foreign investment, and the large number of major infrastructure projects, especially in the transport and public utility sectors. The structural reforms in Hungary and the growing importance of the private sector have created a large financing demand which cannot be completely satisfied by sovereign or corporate lending nor exclusively by funds from the domestic banking market. The latter is still characterised by the limited availability of funding, by the short tenor of loans, and by high interest rates.

THE ROLE OF PROJECT FINANCE

Project finance is a type of limited recourse financing that concentrates on the viability of a specific investment project and its anticipated cash flow streams based on fundamentals such as an independent economic unit, a solid equity base, strong project sponsors, risk sharing, the technical and economic feasibility of the project, an experienced management, special security arrangements that provide tangible support to the lenders, etc. The essence of project finance lies in identifying and analysing all project risks and their financial impact, in separating the risks of the particular project from the corporate or country risk, and in allocating the perceived risks among the parties involved in the project.

This basic project finance structure then has to be adapted to meet the specific needs of the client and the host country. These complex and tailor-made packages can include not only typical project financing elements, but also features from traditional financings such as straightforward loans based on the credit-worthiness of the project company or project sponsors, working capital facilities, capital market transactions, commercial paper issues, leasing, and, primarily for risk mitigation purposes, loans and supplementary credits under export promotion schemes and co-financings with supranational institutions.

Each project requires not only the technical financial skills of the lenders, but also a great deal of creativity in order to come up with a viable financial structure for the specific project. Equally important, the bank and project sponsors need to have a thorough understanding of the project environment in terms of legislation, taxation, economic, political and social developments in the host country, as well as authorisations required from local authorities.

Project sponsors and lenders have come to realise that projects in Hungary cannot be financed on a pure cash flow or on a pure asset basis. The cash flows of the project serve as the principal source of debt repayment of the project. However, they have to be backed-up by tangible security such as the underlying assets and revenue streams of the project. At the same time, project loans cannot be fully secured by the assets of a project, since the realisable values of individual project assets upon liquidation in most cases will not entirely cover the outstanding debt unless it is somehow possible to maintain the project as a going concern.

LOCAL CONSIDERATIONS

When creating project finance packages in Hungary the following additional issues also have to be considered:

- The rate of inflation and the exchange rate of the forint should be carefully evaluated in the cash flow analyses (especially in terms of increasing operating and personnel costs), in order to determine whether projected cash flows are sufficient to repay project loans under various scenarios.

- A practical approach to coping with the exchange rate risk is to match the currency of borrowings with the currency of the project's future revenues. This means that in the case of exports of products or services for hard currency, the debt financing should also be raised in the same currency. However, cross-border financings require a number of approvals from the Hungarian National Bank which need to be taken into account when preparing the completion timetable of a specific project.

- The trend towards more domestic-oriented projects in Hungary – ie investments in local infrastructure, public utilities, retail trade and domestic industry – entails a strong need for local financing. At present, many investors still try to avoid local financings due to current high forint interest rates. However, these interest costs should be weighed against the potential exchange rate risk of the forint on a case-by-case basis.

- The failure of specific investment projects or the need to restructure them is often triggered by the lack of adequate working capital financing at project inception. This could lead to additional leveraging at higher interest rates and may jeopardise the success of the entire project. A successful project financing therefore aims at designing a tailor-made financial package that provides for the total financing needs, including both investment and working capital facilities, in order to successfully complete and operate the project.

- The tight monitoring and control of a project should not be terminated upon its start-up. A permanent information and control system that allows both project sponsors and lenders to respond quickly to changing market conditions and unforeseeable developments is essential to ensure that actual results stay in line with project forecasts.

In conclusion, project finance in Hungary combines conventional and innovative financing techniques that consider the specifics of the project, industry, as well as the political, economic and legal environment of the country in order to create a tailor-made financial package.

27

Investment Strategy

KPMG Peat Marwick

Hungary has attracted the lion's share of foreign investments in Central and Eastern Europe. Investors such as Feruzzi, Kraft, Tate & Lyle, Knorr, Unilever and Philip Morris are busy improving productivity, product lines and packaging. Hungary under the old Comecon division of labour was assigned the task of producing buses for the entire region. Now the country exports Suzuki and General Motors cars, as well as motor components for Ford and other multinationals. From real estate to the stock market or venture capital, opportunities are there to be grabbed by the astute investor. Capital inflows are crucial in facilitating structural reform of the economy. But why invest? Before taking the plunge into a tempting new market, pause and think.

STRATEGIC PLANNING

The basic approach to strategic planning for a UK company looking to invest in Hungary should be no different from the one adopted for investments in other countries. Is it to establish market share on the domestic market or to take advantage of Hungary's traditional export markets or strategic position within Central and Eastern Europe? Is it to establish a low cost base and take advantage of a cheap and educated labour force? How will the proposed investment fit in with your overall corporate strategy? What do you want to achieve? What level of control do you want to retain on your activities? Crucial decisions which will have to be addressed include the level of financial commitment, the expected return on investment, the scale of managerial resources available to develop the business and the

acceptable degree of risk and uncertainty. Will it be a manufacturing venture or a trading one?

Do not invest in Hungary just to take advantage of the tax
holidays. The generous tax breaks are to be phased out from the
end of 1993. But if a new set of inventives does replace the
current system, think about how much incentives will cost to
obtain in terms of guaranteed employment or capital outlays. Do
not invest solely to save on labour costs. Savings on wages may
be outweighed by the cost of retraining and the relatively high
costs of social security contributions. Look at industry and world
market conditions. Expect your original assumptions to be
revised to take into account changes in economic conditions and
markets. There are difficulties, but none of them are insur-
mountable.

Hungary's business infrastructure is almost complete. Budapest was the first city in Eastern Europe to reactivate its stock
market. The city is well supplied with foreign banks, while
virtually every major accounting firm and a fair number of legal
firms have set up shop. The environment for doing business is
not too alien, even if the language is.

When comparing an investment in Hungary with one in
another location, there are a number of positive factors:

- positive strides have been made in creating a comprehensive and workable framework for domestic and foreign
  investment alike;

- medium-sized privatisation is progressing;

- the attitude from officials and the public towards foreign
  investors is generally favourable;

- Hungary is an associate member of the EC;

- its foreign currency holdings are continuing to increase;

- it is relatively stable politically and economically;

- the telecommunication system is still poor but improving.

On the down side:

- the republics of former Yugoslavia are at its borders;

- the competition from neighbours is increasing;

- there are bigger markets further to the east;

- populism is growing;

- traditional markets have been lost and newer ones in the West are in recession.

The structure of the investment will depend to a large extent on the presence, the goals of the investment and the sector. Investments can take the form of a joint venture, an acquisition or starting from scratch. Each opportunity must be assessed on its own merits. With mega deals few and far between, a steady flow of medium-sized deals is much safer.

JOINT VENTURES

In Hungary, as elsewhere in Central and Eastern Europe, joint ventures have been the favoured mode of entry. Indeed, until recently they used to provide the only permitted mode of entry. Joint ventures still tend to dominate certain sectors such as manufacturing, usually with a state-owned company as partner and small trading companies, where capital requirements are smaller, with a non-state partner.

Joint ventures allow the foreign investor to tap into the Hungarian partner's knowledge of the business environment and take advantage of a distribution network. This is appropriate where the Hungarian partner makes a contribution to the capital in kind, or where local market knowledge and contacts are useful. Two major points need to be considered carefully when appraising a potential partner – his creditworthiness and financial standing and his capacity to deliver in terms of quality and punctuality.

Make sure there are no other prior commitments. Your interests must be compatible and the objectives clear. To a Hungarian manager, a joint venture means access to capital, technology, a new product range and access to training. He will not necessarily be interested in notions such as a financial return on his investment. He or she may not be used to taking responsibilities, solving problems and collecting debts. The Western partner on the other hand may be looking for market entry and a distribution network. Agree goals honestly and clarify your expectations and those of your prospective partner. The biggest source of failure is lack of preparation and care taken over the contractual agreements. A joint venture may be useful at the beginning, but a joint venture arrangement should not preclude future evolution if interests grow divergent, even if this means buying out your partner.

BUYING A COMPANY

Although Hungary's privatisation programme has been piece-meal it has covered a wide range of industries including food, tobacco, paper, brewing and manufacturing. The only sectors left relatively untouched have been the utilities such as oil and gas, transport and telecommunications.

One of the characteristics of the Hungarian economy was the dominance of virtual monopolies on particular segments of industrial production. If the company has strong market share and with strong local brand recognition, for a relatively low price it is possible to buy that market share. In 1989, the US conglomerate General Electric purchased a 75 per cent share of the Hungarian light bulb manufacturer Tungsram. This gave GE 7 per cent of the West European market, but markets are not static. Competition from imports will take advantage of the company's rigidity, inflexibility and lack of focus while the privatisation process is going on.

Privatisation does not involve a uniform process for all companies. The State Property Agency (SPA), the organisation handling the privatisation of companies, believes in a case-by-case approach to privatisation, thereby optimising the process. This can be:

- initiated by the SPA, with companies invited to tender for companies on its books;

- initiated by the buyer, having identified a target company (as was the case with Unilever and Feruzzi's acquisition of Kecskemedt); or

- self-privatisation, initiated by the management, with sometimes a foreign investor in mind, in which case the foreign investor who has already started negotiations with the target is in a better position to make a realistic bid and often comes out on top.

The winning bid is only an outline strategy plan. Detailed negotiations, which may take months, only start once the winner has been chosen. Highly visible transactions can become clouded by political considerations. Negotiations are conducted from across the divide of 40 years of a divergent culture. The same knowledge of concepts and words should not be taken for granted. Understand the SPA's agenda. Your interests and those of the SPA are not necessarily incompatible. Patience and flexibility are required.

There are many reasons for being anxious. The lack of reliable information about target companies, means that comparisons remain difficult. The extent to which the SPA is willing to guarantee this information or give indemnities can make or break a deal. Take a commercial approach, otherwise you may end up becoming bogged down in a slow and acrimonious process. SPA will be just as anxious when dealing with warranties, indemnities and claw-back arrangements.

Establishing title to the assets is usually straightforward. However entries in the land register tend to be unreliable. A factory and the land on which it is built may belong to different parties. Existing contractual arrangements should be looked into carefully – there may be a web of pre-existing obligations such as employee agreements and agreements with other parties that may destroy the commercial logic of the exercise. Centrum, a chain of stores, was included in the government's first privatisation programme in September 1990. In the summer of 1992, Kaufring of Germany offered Ft2.5 for a 51 per cent stake. But the bid fell through because Kaufring and the SPA could not agree on employment levels and future disposal of assets.

Look forward rather than backwards. Assess the production facilities, the quality of the goods and the labour force, and estimate how much it will cost to upgrade. You also need to talk to more people than you would in similar circumstances in the West. Be sure you talk to line managers who will give you an indication about how much retraining will be needed.

- Do not underestimate the costs involved, not only the acquisition cost but also the time and costs required to restructure and turn around companies, and also costs involved in updating the technology or marketing facilities.

- The issue of labour is very sensitive and needs to be addressed at the beginning of negotiations.

- Environmental liabilities may be significant.

- Consider product liabilities if the goods are exported.

Build relationships. Néstlé Hungaria operated for 20 years licensing production. Now it has achieved a turnover of Ft9 billion via acquisitions of shares in its former licensees. BAT had links for almost 20 years with the tobacco factory in Pécs, which produced some of its brands under licence. The factory at Pécs underwent spontaneous privatisation and actively sought its own partner. Historic links though are no guarantee of success. R J Reynolds was outbid by the German firm Reemtsma to take over the third largest cigarette factory in Hungary, based at Debrecen in the north-east of the country. Debrecen was one of R J Reynolds' licensees.

A relatively new aspect will be the opportunities offered by the bankruptcy procedures. If the liquidators and other professionals act expeditiously, this could contribute significantly to the privatisation efforts.

GREENFIELD INVESTMENTS

Are greenfield investments a better option? Many investors have avoided the privatisation route altogether and set up greenfield production facilities. Often this is simply because no suitable partner was found rather than as a result of a deliberate choice. The industry may not have been established or highly special-ised facilities may have been required. A greenfield operation avoids difficulties associated with joint venture partners and the liabilities involved in acquiring an existing company, although obtaining the necessary permits and purchasing land can sometimes require negotiations which are just as awkward as those involved in buying a company. Potential investors may balk at the risk of starting from scratch in a country where supply and distribution networks are still rudimentary.

Companies which need minimal technology in a labour intensive sector will often go for a greenfield investment. Businesses which require specific equipment and technology that cannot be accommodated by existing companies and operations will have to be started from scratch. If the foreign company's product is well known, a greenfield development will be as viable as acquiring a company through privatisation. The more capital intensive the industry, the higher the cost of greenfield investments compared to buying existing facilities and improving the technology.

SUB-CONTRACTING

There are several reasons why Hungary could compete in this increasingly globalised market. Its proximity to West European markets, particularly where transport costs or timely delivery are important, provides an opportunity for manufacturers to reduce costs significantly. Assistance and training may be required to enable the subcontractor meet your specifications.

28

Investment Finance

Creditanstalt-Bankverein

The financial infrastructure of Hungary has undergone a tremendous transformation in the past three to five years. Commercial banks, securities companies, money and capital markets, a stock exchange, banking and securities legislation have all been created. Meanwhile the economic and business environment has also seen substantial changes that have affected the development of the financial markets. Inflation has risen from 10 per cent to 36 per cent and subsequently fallen back to 24 per cent.

Interest rates have followed the inflation rate but there were times when real interest rates were negative and times when the financial markets offered substantial rewards for savers. The savings rate has started to grow and by 1992–93 this allowed the government to finance the fast increasing budget deficit on the domestic market. Nevertheless, financing investment projects on the domestic market is still an extremely difficult and cumbersome process and there are very few options available for corporations.

THE LOAN MARKET

The Hungarian banking system can be broken down into three categories of banks:

1. The large, mostly state-owned commercial banks, which have inherited substantial amounts of bad debt from the National Bank of Hungary which gave up its domestic commercial banking functions in 1987. This portfolio of bad debts rapidly increased during the next few years due

to the lack of lending experience and to the economic downturn. As a result, the state decided to clean up the portfolios of these banks, starting in 1992 and probably continuing through 1993–94. The risk awareness of the banks has now greatly increased, and the financing of investment projects is looked at with extreme caution.

2. The newly established foreign commercial banks have so far mostly restricted themselves to working capital financing, and only a few more established banks have ventured into the medium-term market (although generally restricting themselves to financing the subsidiaries or joint ventures of large international corporations).

3. The smaller Hungarian-owned commercial banks have generally not made an impact on the medium to long-term loan market.

THE CAPITAL MARKET

The Hungarian bond market has gone through some hectic times during the past few years in line with the fast changing inflation and interest rates situation. This has meant that at times bonds could be sold in large amounts while during other periods the market practically dried up. Such tendencies are likely to continue until investors experience a more stable inflation and interest rates regime.

The equity market was and is still largely driven by expectations of the further development of the Hungarian economy. Expectations were unrealistically high at the beginning of the 1990s but, during 1993, the market began to revive on a much more sound footing.

Savings and investor mentality

Until the end of the 1980s, savings in Hungary were at relatively low levels, but this situation has changed dramatically in the past few years. Differences between the rich and the poor have substantially increased and unemployment has started to grow relatively fast. These factors contributed to a significant increase in the savings rate despite falling real income levels. Nevertheless, savers still mostly concentrate on short-term instruments like Treasury bills, certificates of deposits and short-term savings deposits. This has put pressure on the banks to try to channel these savings into longer-term, more productive use. Understandably, the banks are acting very cautiously, especially in view of the fast-changing interest rate climate.

Insurance companies and investment funds have started to make their mark during 1993, although the legislation on private pension funds is still waiting for parliamentary approval.

Investment finance in Hungary is reliant on foreign inflows largely denominated in foreign currency. With the development of the financial markets and the stabilisation of the inflation rate this tendency is going to change, introducing the prospect of a much more balanced market.

29

Forming a Company

SJ Berwin & Co

METHODS OF INVESTING

There are many different ways of investing in Hungarian business. The aim of this chapter is to examine the available vehicles and explain how they are formed and controlled. Investment will be considered primarily from the point of view of the need of business people to choose the appropriate vehicle for their proposed investment, whether that be a joint venture through a partnership or limited liability company or a direct investment into an existing company limited by shares.

A brief explanation of the meaning of the term joint venture may be useful at the outset. A joint venture is simply an arrangement where two or more parties come together to participate in an enterprise. It should be distinguished from the frequent references in Hungarian texts to a joint venture being a wholly foreign-owned limited liability company.

Joint ventures can take various different forms. At its most basic it can consist simply of a contractual agreement between two parties to co-operate in a particular way, and in that instance a joint venture will consist of a joint venture agreement which will principally set out the scope of the joint venture and what the rights and obligations of each of the parties are in respect of it. The provisions of the Civil Code on contract law (and perhaps the Foreign Trade Law) will govern such an arrangement.

Alternatively, a joint venture can be established by the formation of a company in which each of the joint venture parties will invest in shares. In the absence of any express agreement, the relationship between the parties who are shareholders in the company will be governed by the constitution of the company and the underlying law in relation to economic associations. This will not normally be satisfactory and therefore it is desirable to have a shareholders' agreement between the shareholders which will set out various matters that govern the relationship beween the joint venturers.

The exact form and content of such an agreement will depend upon the purpose and circumstances of the joint venture but certain provisions covering the duration of the joint venture agreement, management of the company, transfer of shares and resolution of disputes are likely to follow the generally accepted approach. Perhaps the most important aspect in relation to the management of the company would be those matters that could only be undertaken by the joint venture company with the unanimous agreement of all the shareholders.

Although there is no reason why the joint venture company could not be either a limited liability company or a company limited by shares, as will become apparent later in this chapter, the flexibility of the limited liability company will make it the more appropriate vehicle.

It is possible to undertake a joint venture by way of a partnership either in the form of unlimited or limited partnership, but this may not be especially attractive to the investor because of the unlimited liability. A partnership has the additional disadvantage that it is slightly more difficult to bring in new parties and substitute existing parties to the joint venture, and it does not provide an entity through which the business can be conducted.

The rules relating to all forms of economic association are contained in the Business Societies, Associations, Companies and Ventures Act (Act VI of 1988), commonly referred to as the Company Act. There are six types of business association, as follows:

- unlimited partnerships;
- limited partnerships;
- business associations;
- joint ventures;
- limited liability companies; and
- companies limited by shares.

GENERAL PROVISIONS ON BUSINESS ASSOCIATIONS

Creation and registration

The central regulatory body is the Court of Registration which has the final view on the suitability of any proposed corporate entity. To create a business association a founding document, or memorandum and articles of association in the case of a company, must be signed by all the members or shareholders and certified by a notary or a lawyer. It must then be registered at the Court of Registration, which must be notified of any changes in the deed within 30 days of their being made. The entity is deemed to be created once it is registered in the Companies Register.

Business associations (of all forms) may be founded by the state, legal entities and business organisations which are not legal entities or natural persons (the latter including foreign nationals). The same parties may also acquire an interest in associations after their formation. No government consents are required for the acquisition by a foreigner of more than a 50 per cent interest in the business association. In addition, under the Foreign Investment Act, part of the profits belonging to the foreign party can be freely repatriated in the currency of investment without restriction.

A business association can only carry on banking or insurance activities where it is established as a joint stock company.

Executive officers

The executive officers are, in the case of a limited liability company, the managers and, in the case of a company limited by shares, the board of directors. They are elected by the general meeting for a maximum period of five years. They may be re-elected or removed at any time in accordance with the applicable provisions of the Company Act. Executive officers may not be members of the supervisory board.

The supervisory board

The Company Act contains a requirement for certain limited liability companies (where the capital of the company exceeds Ft20 million or the number of members exceeds 25), for any company when the number of employees exceeds an annual average of 200 and for all companies limited by shares, to establish a supervisory board. The supervisory board is generally elected by the company general meeting except in the case of a company limited by shares that has more than 200 employees, in which case one-third of the board comprises employee representatives. Although it has some influence, the supervisory board does not exercise management control. The members of the supervisory board are appointed for not more than five years and can be re-elected or removed at any time in accordance with the applicable provisions of the Company Act.

The members of the supervisory board and the executive officers can be held liable for the default of the company where this stems from a breach of their own duties. The supervisory board can only function when there are two-thirds of members (at least three individual members) present. Votes of the board are carried by simple majority. The supervisory board has the right to examine all the company's books and to require the submission of reports by the executive officers.

Auditors

The deed of association or articles of association can provide that the supervision of the management of the business association may be by an auditor in addition to or instead of the supervisory board.

An auditor must be appointed by a company limited by shares, a single-member limited liability company and a limited liability company with capital in excess of Ft55 million. Auditors must be registered chartered accountants and must not be founders, shareholders or executive officers of the association. A former employee of the company may not act as an auditor within three years of having left.

The auditor has the right to scrutinise all the association's books and to request information from the executive officers. Where an auditor detects a significant decrease in the capital of the company he must notify the supervisory board or, in the absence of such, the shareholders. Where the association does not have a supervisory board the functions of the auditor are similar to the functions of a supervisory board. The auditor may also attend all meetings of the association's supervisory board and executive officers. His principal function is to examine the balance sheet and the register of assets held by the association.

Auditors are appointed for a period of not more than five years and can be re-elected or removed at any time in accordance with the applicable provisions of the Company Act.

Execution of documents

The persons entitled by registration of their signatures with the Court of Registration may sign on behalf of the association. An executive officer alone may sign on behalf of the association. Alternatively, two employees registered with the Court of Registration can sign on the association's behalf.

Regulation by the Court of Registration

All associations are regulated by the Court of Registration. Any of the participants may require the Court to revise a decision of the association where that decision infringes some rule of law or the deed of association or articles of association. This right of automatic recourse does not apply to a participant who has affirmed the decision by a vote, unless this was done by mistake or because of fraud or duress. The action is brought against the association itself within 30 days of the taking of the decision. The court is empowered to prevent the execution of the decision.

Winding-up

The following are the grounds on which winding-up of a business association may take place:

- where any specified period in the deed of association or articles of association for the duration of the association has expired;

- where the association decides to wind itself up without nominating a successor;

- where the association transforms itself into another form of corporate entity;

- where the number of shareholders has been reduced to one;

- where the Court of Registration has liquidated or dissolved the association; and

- the association can be wound-up by either the executive

officers or some other person nominated by the Court if one-tenth of the shareholders so desire.

There are also detailed procedures for the bankruptcy and liquidation of business associations contained in the Bankruptcy and Liquidation Procedures Act (Act IL of 1991).

UNLIMITED PARTNERSHIPS

Unlimited partnerships which must be registered with the Court of Registration do not possess legal personality and as such may be an unattractive vehicle for the foreign investor contemplating a joint venture. The foreign business person contemplating the establishment of a joint venture in the form of a partnership should be aware of the following principal characteristics:

- They have unlimited liability, although liability is two-tiered in that the creditor first looks to the partnership property and only when that is exhausted can he look to the personal property of the partners.

- There is no restriction upon the number of partners nor the amount of capital of the partnership.

- Capital contributions may be in cash or kind. The value of contributions in kind must be stated in the deed of association. Parties making a contribution in kind remain liable for five years from the date of such contribution for any shortfall in the value of the contribution.

- Profits and losses and distributions upon winding-up will be stated in the deed of association.

- Management of the partnership will be regulated by the deed of association. Other partners may bind the partnership. Managers may be changed by a two-thirds majority vote for an 'important reason'.

- Decisions on matters outside the usual business activities of the partnership and alterations to the deed of association require unanimity.

- A partner may withdraw from the partnership upon three months notice, although this may be varied by the deed of association.

- A partner may be excluded from the partnership by a two-thirds majority vote for an 'important reason' (eg breach of statutory or contractual obligations, misconduct jeopardising the objectives of the partnership or insolvency). An excluded partner is entitled to repayment of his partnership interest.

- In the case of a three-partner firm, the expulsion of a partner requires the unanimous resolution of the other two.

- A partner's interest ceases on death or termination, including the liquidation of a corporate partner.

- Partners departing the partnership shall bear for five years from the cessation of the partnership the same liability as the existing partners for debts incurred by the partnership prior to association.

LIMITED PARTNERSHIPS

An alternative to the unlimited partnership is the limited partnership. This type of partnership comprises partners who have limited liability and those who do not, but generally the same rules as an unlimited partnership apply. However, this form has its drawbacks because the Company Act imposes certain controls on the arrangements:

- limited partners may not participate in the management of the partnership;

- a limited partner may lose his protection if his name is included in that of the partnership;

- all partners have a vote on matters outside the usual business activities of the partnership;

- if all limited partners resign, the partnership will continue as an unlimited partnership;

- the partnership comes to an end if all the general partners either die or otherwise terminate the deed of partnership; and

- without the permission of the limited partners the register shall not divulge the identity of the limited partners.

Although the limited liability aspect of such a partnership may be initially attractive to foreign investors, not being able to participate in the management of the business will be a drawback in the emerging Hungarian economy.

BUSINESS UNIONS AND JOINT ENTERPRISES

The business union and the joint enterprise are particular types of associations, apart from companies and partnerships, which are recognised by the Company Act. Both have unlimited liability and are formed by legal entities, in the case of a business union to promote non-economic activity and in the case of a joint enterprise to promote economic activity. It is not thought that foreign investors will find either of these attractive business vehicles.

LIMITED LIABILITY COMPANIES

Formation and share capital

Limited liability companies are in substance very similar to private companies in the United Kingdom in that they cannot offer securities to the public. The minimum number of shareholders is one and therefore it can be a single member 'one person company'. The minimum capital requirement is Ft1 million. The share capital can be paid in cash or in kind, but the minimum contribution on formation of the entity is the higher of Ft500,000 or 30 per cent of the registered capital. The initial capital contributions may not be less than Ft100,000 per shareholder and each contribution must be exactly divisible by Ft10,000. Initial capital contributions must be paid up within one year of registration.

Contributions in kind may be an asset with any real value, intellectual property or any other valuable right. Where the company is required to have an auditor, a higher value than that given by the auditor may not be given to the property. A shareholder contributing in kind possesses a liability for five years for any shortfall in the value of the property.

Structure

The structure of a limited liability company and the relationship between its owners are governed primarily by the contractual terms of the articles of association. The members are free to determine the amount of initial capital contributions, voting rights and the company's management and decision-making structure.

The Company Act contains certain provisions designed to maintain the company as a company with a limited number of shareholders. Shareholders are granted a right of first refusal over other shareholders' shares. Shares may only be transferred to a non-member if the member has paid his primary contribution in full. A shareholder may be excluded by a 75 per cent majority of the general meeting where he has not satisfied his liabilities or is a threat to the objectives of the company.

Corporate organs

General meeting

Within the company the shareholders' general meeting is the primary source of power. The meeting must be held annually. Most decisions are taken by a simple majority of votes, although certain matters require the approval of a three-quarters majority of the shareholders. While the general meeting has the authority to intervene in the functions of other corporate organs, there are a number of functions which are within its own jurisdiction. These include:

- ratification of the annual accounts;

- the conduct of business between the company and the shareholders in that capacity;

- the expulsion and appointment of company officers;

- alterations to the articles of association; and

- the winding-up of the company.

Shareholders may be represented by proxy. For a quorum 50 per cent of the votes must be represented in person or by proxy, or where that percentage of the shareholders responds to a draft resolution circulated to them by the directors. However, shareholders are precluded from voting on any matter that relates to their own business interests.

The manager(s)

One or more managers elected for a fixed period are charged

with the management of the company and represent the company in its relations with third parties. If there are several managers they manage jointly. The manager implements the business policy and takes management decisions. He or she must be an individual but need not be a member of the company. The first manager is appointed in the deed of association. A 50 per cent majority of the general meeting is required to remove a manager.

A manager is not permitted to have business interests which conflict with the interests of the company, although this provision can be excluded by the agreement of the shareholders.

Supervisory board and auditor

A supervisory board must be established where there are more than 25 shareholders, or the share capital exceeds Ft20 million, or the number of full-time employees exceeds 200. In the case of a one-person company the establishment of a supervisory board is only required where the number of employees exceeds 200.

The supervisory board must comprise at least three members. The board is appointed by the general meeting except for the first members who are named in the articles of association. A 75 per cent majority of the general meeting is required to dismiss a member of the board. The board has no management function and, as a result, the manager is the supreme executive body.

The appointment of an auditor is mandatory in the case of a single-member company and a limited liability company with capital in excess of Ft55 million.

Winding-up of the company can only take place, other than by order of the Court, with the agreement of 75 per cent of the shareholders.

JOINT STOCK COMPANIES AND COMPANIES LIMITED BY SHARES

Shares and share capital

In contrast to limited liability companies, joint stock companies are designed to be an organisation owned by the public. Although this form of company will be of little interest to the business people contemplating a joint venture, it is of course relevant to those wishing to make a direct investment in an existing company.

As joint stock companies are open to investment by the public they are subject to greater regulation and possess less structural flexibility. As a consequence, many of the matters left flexible in the formation of a limited liability company are specifically prescribed by the Company Act and may not be altered by agreement.

The minimum share capital is Ft10 million, of which the minimum cash contribution must not be less than Ft5 million or 30 per cent of the total registered share capital. A shareholding in a joint stock company is evidenced by share certificates issued by the company. The formal requirements for the shares are strictly regulated by the Company Act and there are certain items which must appear on certificates. Additionally, further requirements for the public issue of shares have been imposed by the Act on Securities and the Stock Exchange.

There are basically two types of shares – registered and bearer shares. Shares are freely transferable but it should be recalled that a foreign investor may only hold registered shares. The company is required to maintain a share register and therefore any dealings in the company's registered shares must be notified to it. In addition, the Company Act introduced certain special classes of shares:

- Preference shares, the holder of which is entitled to distributable profit prior to other classes of shareholder. The rules as to preference will be contained in the company's articles of association. The value of preference shares may not exceed one-half of the capital of the company.

- Depreciating shares, which pass into the ownership of a public body at a point in time stated in the articles. When this occurs the public body is only entitled to the par value of the shares and the shareholder is entitled to the difference.

- Employee shares, which must be registered and are only transferable between employees and retired employees of the company.

- Interest-bearing shares, entitling the shareholder to a predetermined rate of interest even when there is no profit. Such shares may not exceed 10 per cent of the capital of the company.

- Convertible bonds, which may be issued up to a maximum of one-half of the registered capital.

- Pre-emption bonds, giving holders a right of first refusal on the issue of new shares.

Subscription and formation

As stated earlier, issuing securities (including the content of prospectuses) is regulated by the State Securities Supervision. The Company Act requires the provision of a draft memorandum of association which must include certain specified basic information relating to the company. The Act on Securities and the Stock Exchange enlarges the disclosure requirements. Subscription for shares takes place on signature of the subscription form, following which subscribers are bound by their contractual offer. Ten per cent of the nominal value of the shares must be paid up initially and a general meeting of shareholders must be convened within 60 days of the closing date for subscriptions. This original meeting approves the memorandum of association, elects the board of directors, the supervisory board and the auditors for the first year and takes decisions on other matters required by the Company Act.

Corporate organs

The organs of a joint stock company are as follows:

- the general meeting;
- the board of directors;
- the supervisory board; and
- the auditor.

General meeting

The general meeting is the principal organ of the company. It takes decisions on all matters within its exclusive jurisdiction as stated in the Company Act or the memorandum of association. Resolutions are passed by a majority vote, other than certain important decisions that require a 75 per cent majority. These are:

- alterations to the memorandum of association;

- increases and reductions of capital;

- alterations to class rights attaching to shares; and

- decisions on merger and liquidation.

Board of directors

The board of directors is the managing body of the company and represents the company in its dealings with third parties. The board must consist of at least 3 and not more than 11 directors. The members of the board manage the company jointly. Various other specific tasks are allocated to the board by the Company Act – for example, preparing the annual report and accounts for shareholders. There are provisions in the Company Act forbidding directors from entering into a contract where there may be a conflict of interest.

Supervisory board and auditor

All joint stock companies must have a supervisory board comprising at least three members. Where there are 200 or more employees, one-third of the board must be elected by the employees. The board may convene general meetings of shareholders if the interests of the company require it.

Joint stock companies must appoint an auditor. The rules applying to auditors have been explained earlier in this chapter.

Part IV
Case Studies

Case Study 1

McVitie's

Some consultants and business people argue that the markets in Central and Eastern Europe are so small that the only reason to invest there is to buy low-cost production facilities for exporting to the EC. One company which disputes this line of reasoning is McVitie's, a subsidiary of the £3 billion turnover United Biscuits group. McVitie's has just opened a £4 million factory in Gyor, in western Hungary, which makes crisps for the Hungarian market. And as business development director Andrew Easdale emphasises, the output is not targeted at the wealthy elite – the factory is a true mass-producer. It is the largest British food manufacturing investment in Hungary, and the first British greenfield manufacturing investment there.

INVESTMENT APPRAISAL

McVitie's started investigating the possibilities of investing in Hungary in late-1989 when the company's regional MD visited the country's two major biscuit manufacturers. He was impressed by one, the Keksz company in Gyor (Gyori Keksz), and less than impressed with its rival. During his tour of the latter's factory, a problem arose in the wrapping section. Instead of rushing to solve the problem, or at least shut the production line down, the staff allowed biscuits to pour all over the floor for nearly half an hour.

At Gyori Keksz, by contrast, the manufacturing operation ran smoothly and efficiently, and the management was thinking ahead about how to present their firm to Western investors so that it could survive in the post-communist era. The company was also taking advantage in fairly sophisticated ways of some of the anomalies in the existing legislative regime: for instance, a tax loophole was exploited by the fact that much of the plant was owned by the company's pension fund and the staff canteen. Another important consideration for McVitie's was their strong impression that the Gyori Keksz managers were interested in the long-term future of the firm, not in getting rich quick themselves.

After thorough discussions and negotiations, McVitie's joined Gyori Keksz managers and SPA, the Hungarian privatisation agency, in presenting a privatisation plan to the work-force. Andrew Easdale says the work-force appreciated their honesty when McVitie's admitted that everything would not become wonderful the day after they bought the company, nor even the day after that, but that within five years the staff would notice great improvements as the Hungarian economy picked up and allowed Gyori Keksz to achieve its full potential.

McVitie's bought Gyori Keksz in April 1991 for £11.6 million. The company holds a 50 per cent share of the Hungarian biscuits market, and 60 per cent of wafers. Biscuit consumption in Hungary has some way to go to reach Western European levels, which allows scope for McVitie's to develop the business. Andrew Easdale described the Hungarian biscuit market as one where tastes are as yet largely unformed. Four types of biscuit have traditionally been available: semi-sweet rich tea; sweeter biscuits such as shortcakes; cream biscuits; and decorated biscuits, usually with some form of powdered chocolate added to the surface. Hungarian wafers are apparently high-quality products, but the traditional biscuits are unlikely to impress Western consumers. 'Novel' items such as Jaffa cakes sell extremely well in Hungary.

The new crisp-making plant was built and opened in less than eight months. Initially it is making crisps under the Croky name, a European brand which originated in Belgium. In the longer term the factory will introduce a range of savoury snacks. The new factory was built with the aid of staff from KP, another member of the United Biscuits group. Although McVitie's is focused on biscuits and KP on savoury snacks, they sometimes allocate businesses by geography rather than by product category. Thus McVitie's manages certain snack ranges in Central and Eastern Europe, while KP looks after some biscuit brands in the Asia-Pacific region.

MARKETING THE PRODUCT

Advertising and marketing in Hungary present an interesting challenge. Many Hungarians are very cynical, believing that if a firm needs to make an effort to sell a product it must be of inferior quality. Many of them also associate advertising with the blatant propaganda of the communist era: where previously they were exhorted to cut down their consumption of certain products in order to help buy a tank for Cuba, now they are exhorted to step up their consumption of certain products in order to achieve a Western lifestyle.

But Andrew Easdale reports that most Hungarians understand the role of advertising and promotion in a market economy, and they react well to advertising and other communications which are presented in a sympathetic way. McVitie's adverts are produced in Hungarian by the local office of Leo Burnett's, and he warns against the practice of dubbing Western ads into Hungarian. Apart from the danger of poor dubbing giving a sloppy and unprofessional impression, many Hungarians are concerned that their culture will soon disappear under a tidal wave of American images and icons (even if the companies using them are usually German).

Packaging can be a major problem. Good print quality has not been readily available in Hungary, and McVitie's has imported much of its packaging from Italy (where print costs are often quite low) and also sometimes from Belgium.

The danger of political instability is something that all firms must consider when entering new markets. But when asked about the company's views on the influence of right-wing nationlists in Hungary, or the instances of former communists being re-elected in Poland and Lithuania, Andrew Easdale's first response is laconic: 'people gotta eat!' He goes on to point out that there is a very large measure of agreement that the transition to a market economy is essential, and that certain painful fiscal and monetary disciplines are inevitable. Obviously it would be possible for a radical new government to make life very difficult for McVitie's – a 100 per cent tax on profits would be a good way to start! But even if hotter heads do win more political power, the need to maintain the broad approval of the IMF will restrain their wilder impulses.

Andrew Easdale has no hesitation in recommending Hungary

as an investment location to other British companies. His main advice is to be flexible: do not try to make the Hungarians behave exactly like the British or the Germans. Some established practices need to be changed, but others can be retained in order to preserve elements of the traditional Hungarian way of life. Every company needs plans to guide its business development, but successful ones in Central and Eastern Europe avoid being too rigid.

Case Study 2

Coats Hungary Ltd

Prior to 1939, Coats held a significant share of the market for thread in Eastern Europe with a chain of production bases throughout the region. Following the liberalisation of the region's economies in 1990, Coats Viyella has re-established a factory in Budapest with the objective of reclaiming market leadership throughout Eastern Europe.

Quality in Coats' Budapest factory is now as high as anywhere in Western Europe with a significant cost advantage. Half of the factory's output is exported and production is scheduled to rise by a quarter in 1994.

The new company is benefiting from the flow of cut-make-trim contracts that international design houses, such as Hugo Boss, Max Mara, Liz Clayborne and Patrice Bréal, are placing with local suppliers; as much as 80 per cent of Hungary's garment production is presently being exported to the west.

In the medium-term, the low cost base in Hungary has implications for Coats's overall European strategy. With garment production moving east, not just to Hungary, but to countries with even lower costs such as Russia and Ukraine, the Budapest factory will increasingly become a centre for value-added activities.

BUYING BACK INTO THE MARKET

Coats's original sewing thread mill at Ujpest in Budapest was built in 1926. In 1940 the British managers had to withdraw, entrusting the company to a Hungarian team. In 1942 the company was declared enemy property and run by the government until the mill was occupied by Soviet troops in January

1945. Shortly afterwards the Danube burst its banks and Ujpest stood under a metre of water for several days, suffering extensive damage.

The mill was handed back to Coats at the end of 1945 and its fortunes enjoyed a steady revival until nationalisation by the communists in 1949. At the end of the 80s direct contacts were established with the Hungarian state spinning group, Masterfil, with initial talks directed towards trade agreements. Following the visit of a Coats surveying team to Ujpest, consideration was given to a direct investment. The twisting machines were found to be state-of-the-art German units, although spinning machines were closer to a 1926 vintage!

A 60/40 joint venture was agreed with Masterfil in November 1990. Shareholdings were determined by obtaining external valuations of the land, buildings and machinery and multiplying this by 1.5 to determine a capital injection of approximately $10m by Coats. This was spent entirely on new machinery. 'The result is that the Ujpest mill is probably the most modern sewing thread production unit in Europe,' comments Nick Langford, Managing Director of Coats Eastern Europe. 'It has no difficulty in matching – and usually surpassing – West European quality levels.'

Dealing with the bureaucracy is often cited as a particular difficulty in setting up and running a joint venture. 'It is more of a minor hindrance, than a serious obstacle', comments Nick Langford. 'While there are delays, we have not encountered serious corruption in Hungary, which is remarkable in a country where officials are relatively poorly paid.'

OPERATIONAL CONSIDERATIONS

Nick Langford arrived three months before the joint venture was due to go live. He recalls that, 'the task of recruiting a management team, installing computer systems, developing a service culture and modernising the entire production facilities seemed enormous.'

Coats's joint venture partners, Masterfil, took time to adjust to the role of minority shareholder. 'It came as a bit of a shock to find that the annual budget or business plan was not subject to their veto.' Using a business plan as a flexible framework within which to work also came as a surprise. A clearer understanding has now developed and the possibility of a second joint venture is under discussion.

At Ujpest, the strength of the existing Hungarian management team lay in production, so key appointments had to be filled. A local Sales and Marketing Director, who had gained four years commercial experience in New York, was recruited. A Hungarian Finance Director, who had processed World Bank loans at a state owned rubber enterprise, was also brought in. Both, therefore, were already attuned to Western financial disciplines, although they have since undergone further training with the help of the Know How Fund.

In addition to Nick Langford, two further expatriates have been working in the finance and operations departments. However, they have had Hungarian understudies, who are due to take over in 1994.

Over two years the workforce has been reduced from around 500 to 420, although there has been no need to carry out compulsory redundancies. Wage pressures are limited, although managers' salaries are a different matter. 'There is a heavy demand for people with the right skills,' reports Nick Langford. 'However, anyone prepared to invest in training Hungarian staff stands to reap huge benefits.'

BUSINESS DEVELOPMENT

At the Ujpest factory, Coats had to establish a marketing operation from scratch. Its sales team of eight is backed up by a technical advisory service, as well as a computerised forecasting programme which it is running in partnership with its largest and most reliable customers. The intention is to find ways of responding as quickly as possible to the volatile specifications of international design.

Although wages in Hungary are currently about one eighth of German levels, pay in some parts of the CIS is currently only a tenth of Hungarian levels.

It is likely therefore that production of grey thread, essentially a commodity item, will tend to move still further east from Budapest to Russia or the Ukraine. Value added activities, such as the dyeing and finishing of thread, will be concentrated at Ujpest (which hopes to introduce ISO 9000 during 1994).

Case Study 3

Watmoughs

During 1990, Hungary was selected by Watmoughs (Holdings) PLC as the location for its first overseas investment and this led to the creation of a new business, initially in partnership with Hungarian State companies on 1 February 1991. After establishing itself as one of the UK's largest printing groups with particular strengths in long-run quality magazines (such as *Harpers & Queen*, and newspaper supplements like *You* magazine for *The Mail on Sunday*), Watmoughs was looking for its future growth outside the highly competitive domestic UK market. The strategy adopted during 1990 was to enter a domestic European market by way of a relatively modest acquisition in Central Europe and to explore the possibility of a major investment in Spain.

Competition in Western European countries was as fierce as in the UK. The only apparent opportunity for major investment offered itself in Spain, provided that enabling contracts with major publishers could be secured. For a more speculative and smaller-scale investment the company's attention was drawn to the emerging markets of Central Europe, not least because Western European and British publishers were entering those markets creating a demand for service and quality. In addition, privatisation promised to create a new demand for annual reports and other corporate literature.

Hungary rapidly emerged as the principal target, as several leading Western publishers were already getting involved. It was located close to potential export markets in Western Europe (particularly Austria) and was establishing a reputation as a stable environment for Western investors.

INVESTING IN HUNGARY

With the help of David Kirkby, an accountant turned media professional who had already negotiated the acquisition of Hungary's leading regional newspaper for Associated Newspapers, Watmoughs looked more closely at opportunities to invest in existing printing companies being prepared by the state for privatisation. Six were listed and all were visited during a short tour arranged in 1990. The best opportunity was deliberately placed last on the list and was of immediate interest.

Revai Nyomda was a state-owned general printing company based in Budapest and equipped with sheet-fed presses, serving high quality publishing and fine art markets. Turnover in 1990 was £1.6 million and the company employed 140 people. Watmoughs was particularly impressed with Revai's go-ahead management style. The company was in the process of supplementing its existing printing and binding capacity with a new web offset press. The company had sold its part ownership of a city centre site and identified as a suitable new location a partly completed sports hall in a suburb of Obuda.

These developments were beyond the financial resources of Revai Nyomda and the company was seeking an outside investor through the State Property Agency (SPA). By bringing in its marketing and technical skills, as well as new finance, Watmoughs saw scope for developing Revai Nyomda as a leading printer of high quality newspaper products, magazines and product brochures in the Hungarian and adjacent markets.

At the beginning of February 1991, Watmoughs acquired 57 per cent of Revai Nyomda for £2.3 million, with the state retaining 43 per cent. On reflection, David Kirkby concedes that 'the price for Revai was probably higher than we would have wanted to pay, but we did not want to see negotiations go on interminably with SPA'.

As the business moved into profit in 1992, and capacity filled, more investment was needed. The state companies were unable to meet the call for an increase in the share capital and, on behalf of Watmoughs, David Kirkby entered into negotiations with SPA to purchase the minority share. Negotiations took a long time because of the state's procedural requirement to seek other offers and for proposals to be based on asset valuations, but in the end the acquisition was completed at a discount, which made the overall investment sensibly priced.

MANAGING THE OPERATION

Revai Nyomda is managed by an Hungarian team and David Kirkby continues to be involved in the business, fulfilling a non-executive and advisory role as chairman of the supervisory board for two to three weeks a month. The staff level initially employed in the new company in 1991 was perhaps 20 per cent higher than a comparable British operation. However, redundancies have been avoided as additional work has been won, further equipment has been installed and productivity levels have improved. New procedures have had to be established. In the past, the company took on new business without much regard to its net profitability, its effect on the production capacity or the credit status of the client.

Installing an efficient estimating system proved a drawn out exercise. In the past, customers had been seen as 'necessary but a nuisance' and estimates could take up to a week or two to produce. Significant improvements have now been made with the introduction of a computerised costing system, and quotations are now usually issued within 48 hours of an inquiry.

The effectiveness of training programmes has varied. The learning curve has been longer than expected: a lifetime of working practices and the language have proved to be significant barriers. 'Bringing in a practical person from the UK to work with the Hungarian crew on a machine has had good results', comments David Kirkby. 'Bring in a manager to advise and they will nod sagely, but nothing will happen. There is a need to lead by example'.

Hungarian employees are enthusiastic learners of quality control systems, often proving too enthusiastic, striving to achieve perfection. Industrial relations in the printing industry are relatively good. Neither the companies nor the employees are well organised in an industry-wide way. Staff terms and conditions are usually covered by an annual collective agreement which is negotiated between management and representatives of the staff. At Revai the staff have proved supportive of the management as the company has grown dramatically. Extra staff have been employed and, as a result of increased productivity, wages (from low rates) have grown faster than the level of inflation.

The structure of the business has not worked out as initially anticipated. In the West, printing has become increasingly specialised: functions like typesetting and film making are put out to specialists. In Hungary it is often still an integrated operation and publishers, familiar with the service, want it to continue. These functions were not acquired in the misplaced hope that the work would be taken up by a new breed of specialists in Hungary. However, the firm has subsequently had to install an Apple Mac typesetting facility. The lack of specialisation means that quality standards are lower than in the West.

TRADING CONDITIONS

The original marketing strategy was to establish Revai in a growing market for prestigious magazines and to pull back quality business that had been going to Austria. In a difficult economic climate, David Kirkby admits that this approach 'took a few knocks, but may now be regarded as successful'.

By working 24 hours a day Austrian printing companies are able to retain a degree of price competitiveness in the face of low labour costs in Hungary. Revai's quality and service are improving and Austria remains a prime export target, along with Poland, where there is limited quality printing capacity. Overall, David Kirkby's medium-term target is for exports to make up 50 per cent of sales.

In Hungary itself, expectations of relatively buoyant pricing levels were undermined by the uncompetitive behaviour of state enterprises. Unburdened by the imperative of cost and profit, they were able to offer cut-throat prices. David Kirkby cites an example of a state gravure printing house. Normally the process is uneconomic if used for runs of less than 300,000 copies. The state enterprise was using it on runs as short as 15,000. There is a positive side to this – in competition with state enterprises it is easier to offer benefits to the customer through good manage-ment and service.

Cash flow is also a problem because clients are often burdened with debt. Revai is therefore concentrating its sales strategy on Western companies, with a particular emphasis on producing brochures and reports for financial services, as well as news-paper supplements for Western publishers operating in Hun-gary.

In spite of these difficulties, Revai Nyomda has been successful in attracting new business. The first rotary press started to operate in February 1991 and by the end of that year work available had almost filled capacity. A second and larger press was installed in the autumn of 1992 and a growing reputation for service and quality ensured that capacity was again full by spring 1993. The original sheet-fed part of the business was enhanced by the installation of a five-colour Heidelberg press on which fast turnround financial documents could be produced to the extremely high quality standard set by the privatisation agencies and financial advisers.

By March 1994 the construction of a new press hall will be completed to house the company's largest press so far, a Baker Perkins G16, capable of producing 32 pages of colour in one revolution. This will start to operate in April. This investment will double the capacity of Revai and the company will be looking more aggressively at domestic markets and for export business.

Watmoughs' faith in the continuing growth of Revai is demonstrated by the investment in the building, which is designed to accommodate a fourth press in due course, with little further expense on construction. The investment in Revai Nyomda has allowed Watmoughs the opportunity to learn how the Hungarian market works. The business has moved steadily towards a satisfactory level of profitability on sales which trebled in the first three years of operation. The company is now well positioned to establish itself as an exporter and, perhaps, to invest elsewhere in the region in due course.

Case Study 4

Andromeda Software

Hungary has a proud tradition in mathematics along with an aptitude for puzzles of all sorts, not least chess. As well as fostering a culture which gave the world the Rubik cube, this tradition has proved a fertile environment for computer programmers, and Hungary has won for itself an honourable place in the history of computer games through the activities of companies such as Andromeda Software.

Following a degree of trade liberalisation in the early 80s, Andromeda found a mechanism to establish itself as a worldforce in developing software for games, licensing its programmes to Sony, amongst others.

Robert Stein, an Hungarian emigré from the 1956 revolution, based in London, was the driving force in the development of the company. 'Hungarians always used to want to go to Germany', he comments. 'My philosophy was that they should not be selling their labour cheaply, but finding ways to sell the results of their intellect, creativity and enterprise'.

Robert Stein's own entrepreneurial career began as a sales engineer in the UK. He went on to set up his own consumer electronics company, distributing Texas Instruments' early calculators and making his reputation with the VAT-man range of calculators.

Introducing chess computers proved harder. High street retailers found them unattractive, as they were new products requiring a dedicated computer and a relatively sophisticated demonstration. However, chess computers did become the first non-photographic product carried by Dixon's, now one of the UK's largest consumer electronics chains.

Setting up dedicated counters in House of Fraser stores, such as 'Futuretronics' and 'Chips with Everything', was more productive. The project then really took off with the introduction of the first consumer computer, the Commodore v20.

With queues of customers at each House of Fraser counter, the need for new software for the Commodore became intense. This search led Robert Stein to return to Hungary in 1982, where a year earlier he had held the first chess computer symposium and met a lot of computer programmers.

It was still a restrictive, controlled economy and the authorities were distrustful of foreign involvement, following the debt crisis of the early 80s. However, there were promising trends.

Flush with the success of the Rubik cube, the Hungarians were looking to foster new ideas and products through a new innovation company, Novotrade, set up in 1982. In addition, the monopolies held by state trade organisations were being challenged by the official introduction of a general trading company, which encouraged a climate in which enterprise could flourish. Many of Hungary's leading entrepreneurs began their careers in the early 80s.

The genesis of Andromeda Software lay in a telex message to Robert Stein, following the chess symposium, from Reny Gabor, a manager at the Scala retail chain: 'I require your presence in the next two weeks to start business together'.

Reny Gabor and Robert Stein found a match between distributing Commodore 64s into Hungary in return for the development of software. Currency restrictions necessitated a relatively complicated trading mechanism. Outstanding payments to Robert Stein were to be settled in hard currency earned by the sales of shoes in Italy, as well as from the revenue from software licensed worldwide.

Under the West's rules governing the entry of technology into the old eastern bloc, the Commodore 64 was the only computer legally allowed in. Over the next three years, 100,000 were to be sold in Hungary.

The development of software took off in parallel, quickly becoming an international force. A team of 100 programmers produced games such as the Spitfire simulator, Eureka and even the first Ninja products. Hungarians worked harder and cost less than their English counterparts according to Robert Stein. 'They were always creative, even when they did not need to be'.

The criticism of games produced in Hungary was that they tended to be too peaceful and too intellectual to have a total appeal. It was also difficult to get programmers attuned to the expectations of international consumers. Developing golf games was the worst of all, as it was a sport virtually unknown in eastern Europe.

From the mid-80s a wide range of opportunities opened up in the domestic Hungarian market. Robert Stein's proposal to publish *The Guinness Book of Records* locally was met with incredulity at first. His reasoning was that Hungarians were desperate for opportunities to express their individualism. '*The Guinness Book of Records* represented everyday folk's chance to become heroes. It was a road to fame.' Fifty thousand copies were sold in the first month!

Robert Stein has since developed a string of joint ventures in other fields. He set up a school to teach executives English and business skills for the Oxford Business Certificate. He holds a stake in a former state company which sells Hungarian *objets d'art* abroad. He runs a publishing company that draws on the experience and expertise of local journalists for international consumption.

Andromeda has had its own office importing and selling computers since 1987. The lifting of import controls radically altered the market. 'Everyone became a wholesaler or importer,' Robert Stein comments. 'The market went to pieces: there were lots of small orders with endless undercutting of prices. Margins were very tight and Hungarians were reluctant to work with middlemen. You can still buy the cheapest computers anywhere in Europe in Hungary'.

'It remains a deceptively open market,' argues Robert Stein. 'Anyone can walk in, but there is no guarantee of finding any customers and setting up a distribution network represents a heavy investment. You have got to have a presence on the ground.'

Although financial conditions have been very tight for ordinary Hungarians, getting paid is not one of the constraints to doing business. The problem that Robert Stein has encountered with his ventures is that Hungarians appreciate neither the importance of the middleman nor of minority shareholders. 'It sometimes seems they would prefer control over an unsuccessful project, than a part share in something which is going places.'

Despite this shortcoming in adapting to the conventions of a free market, Robert Stein is convinced that the change over the past four years in the economy and in people's attitudes is little short of miraculous. He is busy planning the next stage of Andromeda's development in Hungary. In the meantime, Novotrade, one of his original partners, became Hungary's first publicly quoted company with a turnover of $50 million and with Reny Gabor as its chairman.

Appendices

Appendix 1

Opportunities by Sector

British Chamber of Commerce in Hungary

FOOD

The Hungarian food industry is currently one of the best investment targets for expanding companies. It has great traditions, skills and size and an excellent raw material base. Yet because of the recent political and economic upheavals, superb Hungarian companies can be acquired for a fraction of the price of similar ones only a few hundred miles further west.

The agricultural sector is experiencing difficulties, however, as a result of the culmination of subsidy removal on land, ownership uncertainty and poor crop yields for the last two years. Opportunities exist for value-added processors since much of the current exports are sold as commodities.

CONSTRUCTION

Infrastructural opportunities exist, particularly in connection with the proposed construction of toll motorways. The office market is reasonably well served, though scope in the medium term may exist for low-cost housing. The high price of land for new starts will make renovation increasingly attractive.

HEALTH

The state health service is suffering from acute underfunding. This is prompting the development of a number of private facilities. Affordability is the key issue and there may be scope for further insurance offerings and affordable private medical facilities.

TEXTILES

Tremendous opportunities exist for garment manufacturers to do business on a cut, make and trim basis (whereby British principal supplies design + fabric and Hungarian sub-contractor supplies trim and labour). Many manufacturers from other Western European countries have been operating in Hungary (and other Eastern European countries) for many years and have now moved on from purely contractual relationships to take equity holdings in their newly privatised Hungarian partners. UK companies have lagged behind in this area. Other, less labour intensive, sectors of the textile industry in Hungary are not particularly attractive to investors; existing enterprises have suffered from lack of capital investment for 40 years and would now be expensive to re-equip.

ENERGY

Enormous scope for participation in the privatisation of the gas network. Funding has recently been negotiated for the expansion of electricity production from gas. Questions as to the future of the country's nuclear power generating facilities at Paks must also raise longer-term opportunities for either upgrade or decommissioning and replacement. The government is also giving consideration to building a second nuclear power station in the east of the country to ensure dependence on oil and gas pipelines from the Ukraine and other CIS states. On a microscale, increasing fuel costs will yield opportunities for replacement of heating systems and upgrading of insulation.

TRANSPORT

The country remains committed to the provision of efficient, modern public transport. Funds are available for the upgrading of certain rail lines and rolling stock. A programme for engine upgrades for the bus stock is underway. Emphasis in the public transport sector will increase in the areas of fuel efficiency and the reduction of emissions. Some privatisation in this sector is not inconceivable but not a current priority.

Domestic freight networks are poor and many manufacturers struggle with logistics.

ENGINEERING

Audi, GM, Ford and Suzuki have all invested in Hungary. At varying levels they are looking to increase the local component of manufactured units. Traditional engineering skills are very high in Hungary but plant is largely outdated and was focused very much on the heavy engineering demand from other Eastern Bloc countries. Several competent local candidates have been identified for local component manufacture.

CHEMICALS

Hungary is a proven sub-contract manufacturer of speciality chemicals and may also be a valued supplier of scarce raw materials. Both chemical and pharmaceutical sectors are traditionally strong.

ELECTRONICS

Again, good skills among the labour force; a significant amount of software is written in Hungary. In terms of applications, banking and communication sectors would seem to offer the best scope. Vehicle component manufacture may also be attractive.

CONSUMER GOODS

The liberalisation of import controls has resulted in the country being flooded with imported, and expensive, consumer goods. Much domestic capacity is now redundant and unable to compete with the quality standard of imports. Balance of payments pressure may come to bear with a benefit to modernised local production. A number of internationally known branded items are made in Hungary, including Waterford glass and Samsonite luggage, proving that the highest quality standards are achievable.

TOURISM

Still enormous scope for increasing the quality of visits to Hungary. Also, the government is about to commence the sale of over 100 historic properties (lodges, castles, etc) throughout the country. Requiring extensive renovation in many cases, these represent superb potential for country hotel/club-type developments. Medium-grade state-owned hotels may also be of interest. Several excellent Hungarian construction/renovation contractors have been identified.

PROPERTY

Budapest office and premium housing prices are very high. Acute shortage of medium–low-cost housing. Many state-owned flats are now being sold to tenants but come with structural problems. Property agents/management groups are well represented in the market but their service levels vary widely. Premium office space is now well supplied but quality of medium-grade space is poor. Brokers report that attractive deals, yielding 15+ per cent can be negotiated despite high initial asking prices.

SERVICES

Provision of services is generally poor in Hungary. Exceptions are: fast food, most of the big names are here, and courier services, DHL started in 1984. Banking is generally very inefficient and the range of insurance products limited. Scope may exist for the provision of contracted-out services (eg cleaning, catering).

Telecommunication systems are in the process of privatisation. Substantial investment will be required to achieve the growth- and service-level targets which have been set. British interests are currently under-represented in this field.

Appendix 2

Economic Aid Programmes

THE EBRD IN HUNGARY

Established in May 1990, the European Bank for Reconstruction and Development exists 'to foster the transition towards open market-oriented economies and to promote private and entrepreneurial initiative in the Central and Eastern European countries committed to and applying the principles of multiparty democracy, pluralism and market economics' (Agreement establishing the EBRD, Chapter 1, Article 1). The Bank, with initial subscribed capital of ECU10 billion, merges the principles of merchant and development banking. A wide variety of financial instruments are offered by the Bank including loans, equity, guarantees and underwriting.

Since the EBRD's inauguration in 1991, Hungary has been a primary focus of Bank activity. As at the end of 1993, the Bank had approved 24 projects in Hungary, worth ECU644 million, making Hungary the largest recipient of EBRD financing in the region. Funding has been extended to private and privatising enterprises, as well as the public sector. Investments supporting private enterprise have been in various fields including electronics, telecommunications, packaging materials, the automotive industry, chemicals, food, hotels and financial institutions. In addition, the Bank has also provided loans to, and taken an equity stake in, the recently privatised Hungarian telecommunications company, Matav. Key areas which the EBRD is concentrating on currently include the financial sector, privatisation and restructuring, agribusiness and infrastructure.

THE WORLD BANK

The World Bank, the leading global aid agency, began lending to Hungary in 1983, and since then has concentrated its support on assisting the country's efforts at creating a market-based economy.

This support has been provided in three ways: (i) by promoting reforms that encourage private sector activity, such as foreign price liberalisation, the establishment of a clear tax system and the elimination of budgetry support for state enterprises; (ii) by supporting the development of institutions, such as a banking system, that facilitate private sector growth; and (iii) by providing assistance to small and medium-sized enterprises (SMEs).

By 1 June 1993, the Bank had financed 38 loans to Hungary, totalling US$3.4 billion. From the Bank's total commitment, 28 per cent was to industry, 15 per cent to agriculture, 9 per cent to the energy sector, 15 per cent to transport and telecommunications, 12 per cent to human resources development, and the remaining 21 per cent to general balance of payments support.

Two projects to modernise the pensions and social administrations and to upgrade the health services have just been approved. A project to modernise the tax administration system, and one promoting energy conservation, will shortly be presented to the Board for approval. Among other projects being prepared, a roads project has recently been negotiated, and an urban transport project will shortly be appraised.

International Finance Corporation

The International Finance Corporation (IFC) is a World Bank affiliate and the largest source of direct project financing for private investment in developing countries. IFC's share capital is provided by 155 member countries which collectively determine IFC's policies and activities.

Hungary was the first of the Central and Eastern European countries to join IFC in 1985, and IFC opened its Budapest office in 1991. On 30 June 1993, IFC's portfolio and commitments in Hungary amounted to approximately US$150 million. The Corporation has invested in 13 enterprises including Westel (telecommunications), First Hungary Fund (an investment fund) and Unicbank.

In the next 2–3 years IFC aims to expand its investment portfolio, with the emphasis on infrastructure (particularly telecommunications), food processing, distribution and some areas of general manufacturing. IFC also aims to develop mechanisms to assist the SME sector, either through direct investment or in co-operation with a local partner.

PHARE

PHARE is a major G-24 assistance programme to Eastern Europe co-ordinated by the EC Commission. The allocation for the 1993 programme in Hungary was ECU100 million.

Recent programmes

Since 1990 some ECU317 million have been committed on national programmes. In addition Hungary has benefited from regional programmes in the areas of transport, environment, energy, nuclear safety, public administration reform, customs and telecommunications, among others. An approximate break-down of all approved programmes indicates that technical assistance accounts for 41 per cent of cumulative commitments, training for 15 per cent, equipment and supplies for 29 per cent and financial instruments (loan and credit guarantee schemes) for 15 per cent.

Although the programme as a whole straddles many sectors, enterprise development (comprising privatisation, restructuring, SMEs and investment and trade promotion), agriculture and the environment together account for over half of total commitments since 1990. These were also the sectors of primary focus when the programme started.

As of February 1993, the 1991 and 1992 commitments for privatisation, restructuring, SMEs and investment promotion were ECU86 million, of which 33 per cent had been contracted. Commitments to agriculture and the environment accounted for ECU85.5 million, of which ECU48.25 million or 51 per cent had been contracted. Overall, some 41.5 per cent of the ECU317 million committed since 1990 have been contracted.

Medium-term priorities

A rolling two-year perspective has been adopted starting in 1993. The government has decided that PHARE assistance over the medium term should focus on the following broad strategic areas:

- economic development;
- human resources development;
- regional development;
- environmental protection; and
- public administration development.

Planned activities

Agriculture

Agriculture, which accounted for about 18 per cent of GDP in 1990, is undergoing a substantial transformation process. PHARE 1993–94 will support the general restructuring process in the agricultural sector and, with a view to decentralisation and the possibilities of co-financing with Hungarian and other foreign sources, the parties will explore the possibility of channelling part of the assistance through the Agricultural Development Fund.

Enterprise restructuring and privatisation

An increasing number of state-owned enterprises will require some form of restructuring before privatisation can take place. A Special Restructuring Programme co-financed with the EBRD and possibly mobilising other resources is being appraised. A phased programme of support is envisaged with more substantial assistance being made available in 1994 subject to progress in 1993.

SME development

Support for establishing an environment conducive to SME development is given special emphasis by the government. PHARE support from 1993 will include the extension of the regional services network and credit facilities.

Financial sector

Deficiencies in the financial sector remain one of the main bottle-necks to economic development. The PHARE 1991 programme focused on feasibility studies and preliminary technical assistance to develop appropriate strategies and to provide training to key financial institutions. The PHARE 1993 programme in the financial sector will therefore be designed to follow up and consolidate the assistance already being provided.

Technological development and quality management
The insufficient technological development and quality management of most enterprises constitute major technical barriers to trade. The PHARE 1993 programme will support the development of institutions and systems designed to enable them to serve enterprises efficiently.

Euro-GTAF
The Euro-GTAF (General Technical Assistance Facility for the Implementation of the Europe Agreement) was initiated under PHARE in 1992 to support the implementation of the Europe Agreement and prepare Hungary for her gradual integration into the European Communities.

Infrastructure, housing and energy efficiency
Both parties agree that the potential for PHARE assistance in the form of investment or pre-investment support should be explored in such areas as housing development, energy efficiency improvements and infrastructure development Potential for parallel financing with domestic resources, other donors and loan financing from international financial institutions will be explored.

Trade and investment promotion
Based on an assessment of the PHARE 1991 programme and in the context of new institutional arrangements under consideration by the government for promoting trade development and foreign investment, PHARE could provide further support in this area during 1994.

Higher education
New strategic priorities for the restructuring of higher education are being worked out for the next phase of TEMPUS. The provisional budget allocation for 1994 will allow for the timely preparation of projects in relation to the 1994–95 academic year.

Health sector reform
The government's ongoing health reform programme envisages

a shift towards a stronger primary healthcare network. PHARE 1993 will focus on the first level of the healthcare system including institutional strengthening, training and privatisation measures.

Regional development

As the PHARE 1992 programme will be operational only from mid-1993, both parties agree that no additional support should be envisaged from this year's allocation. Recommendations for additional investment-oriented support will be assessed during 1993 as a basis for considering new allocations from the 1994 budget.

Environmental protection

The PHARE 1992 programme in support of the Central Environmental Protection Fund will be operational as from mid-1993. Both parties agree that no additional support is needed from PHARE 1993. Possible further support in 1994 will be assessed late in 1993.

Civil society

Consideration will be given to the feasibility of a specific PHARE scheme to be managed by and for the NGO community.

KNOW-HOW FUND

In 1989 the UK pledged £25 million for Hungary under the Know-How Fund (KHF). Despite its relatively modest size, the KHF has earned a good reputation in Hungary, and is widely appreciated for its quality, speed and flexibility.

The major programmes

Financial sector

The largest single project in Hungary is support for the development of the Accelerated Privatisation Programme (APP). It is designed to significantly speed up the sale of state-owned companies and to widen share ownership amongst Hungarian citizens.

With over £1 million of KHF technical assistance the Budapest Stock Exchange has succeeded in developing and establishing a new trading floor and trading system.

Management training

The KHF has now devoted over £5 million to the development of new high quality management training courses in Hungary.

Small business and employment

The KHF has made a significant contribution to the development of a network of local enterprise agencies to support the growth of small and medium-sized enterprises throughout Hungary. The KHF has provided assistance through the UK Department of Employment with the establishment of an Open Learning Centre in Budapest linked to the employment service.

Public administration/good government

The KHF has funded a major programme of advice and training for local government. A parallel programme in support of the reform of the central civil service is also under way – the Civil Service Training and Development Project.

Industrial Restructuring

The United Nations Industrial Development Organisation (UNIDO) is working up projects to spend the remainder of the total KHF pledge of £1 million to a trust fund for industrial restructuring in Hungary.

Investment support

Some £1.5 million has been offered so far to British firms seeking investment in Hungary. Some 37 grants have been awarded under the KHF Pre-Investment Feasibility Studies (PIFS) scheme and 31 firms have applied successfully for training grants under the Training for Investment Personnel Scheme (TIPS).

Manager attachments

The KHF is also financing a successful British Council/CBI-administered programme enabling Hungarian managers to spend 3 to 4 week attachments with UK companies. Over 50 managers have come since 1991 with a further 120 attachments planned over the 3 years to 1996.

Sources of Further Information

THE CONTRIBUTORS

SJ Berwin & Co
222 Grays Inn Road
London WC1X 8HB
Tel: 44 (71) 837 2222
Fax: 44 (71) 833 2860
Contacts: Michael Rose/
Simon McLeod

Creditanstalt-Bankverein
29 Gresham St
London EC2V 7AH
Tel: 44 (71) 822 2659
Fax: 44 (71) 822 2663
Contacts: John Crocker/
Alfred Taui

ETD Ltd
Maypole House
Maypole Road
East Grinstead
West Sussex
RH19 1HL
Tel: 0342 317770
Fax: 0342 317774
Contact: Peter Tarnóy

KPMG Reviconsult Kft
1122 Budapest
Maros utca 19–21.
Tel: 010 (36) 1 202 2299
Fax: 010 (36) 1 202 4405

Politconsult Budapest
(a subsidiary of GJW
Government Relations
London)
1022 Budapest II.
Bimbó út 1.
Tel: 010 (36) 1 116 3998
    010 (36) 1 135 0747
Fax: 010 (36) 1 135 5792
Contact: Mr Tibor Vidos
Government relations/
lobbyists.

**Saatchi & Saatchi
Hungary**
Alvinci út 16
H-1022 Budapest
Tel: 010 (36) 1 115 4090
Fax: 010 (36) 1 135 5772
Contact: Keith Ginsberg

UNITED KINGDOM

Confederation of British Industry
Centre Point
103 New Oxford Street
London WC1A 1DU
Tel: 44 (71) 379 7400
Fax: 44 (71) 836 1972
Contact: Pauline Shearman, Head, Central & East European Dept., International Affairs Directorate

Department of Trade and Industry
Hungary Desk
Kingsgate House
66–74 Victoria St.
London SW1E 6SW
Tel: 44 (71) 215 5673
Fax: 44 (71) 215 4743
Contact: Simon Evans

Department of Trade and Industry
Export Market Information Centre (EMIC)
Ashdown House
125 Victoria St.
London SW1E 6RB
Tel: 44 (71) 215 5444
Fax: 44 (71) 215 4231

Department of Trade and Industry
World Aid Section
Room 291
Ashdown House
123 Victoria St.
London SW1E 6RB
Tel: 44 (71) 215 6210/44 (71) 215 6089
Fax: 44 (71) 215 6535

East European Trade Council
10 Westminster Palace Gardens
Artillery Road
London SW1P 1RL
Tel: 44 (71) 222 7622
Fax: 44 (71) 222 5359
Contact: JA McNeish – Director

Embassy of the Republic of Hungary
Commercial Section
46 Eaton Place
London SW1X 8AL
Tel: 44 (71) 235 8767
Fax: 44 (71) 235 4319
Contact: Mr Ede Sziklai – Commercial Counsellor

HUNGARY

General

British Embassy
Commercial Section
Budapest V
Harmincad utca 6.
Tel: 010 (36) 1 266 2888
Fax: 010 (36) 1 266 0907

British Chamber of Commerce in Hungary
1011 Budapest
Iskola u. 37. I/4.
Tel/fax: 010 (36) 1 201 9142
Contact: Mrs Éva Márkus – Secretary General

Hungarian Chamber of Commerce
1055 Budapest
Kossuth Lajos tér 6–8
Tel: 010 (36) 1 153 3333
Fax: 010 (36) 1 153 1285
Contact: Mr Sándor Sárecz –
UK Desk Officer

Magyar Joint Venture Szövetség
(Hungarian Joint Venture
  Association, affiliate of
  Hungarian Chamber)
1012 Budapest
Kuny Domokos u. 13–15.
Tel: 010 (36) 1 115 8025
Fax: 010 (36) 1 156 0728
Contact: Dr Iván Toldy-Ösz
  – Director

Nemzetközi Gazdasági Kapcsolatok Minisztériuma
(Ministry of International
  Economic Relations,
  MIER)
H-1055 Budapest V
Honvéd u. 13–15.
Tel: 010 (36) 1 153 0000
Fax: 010 (36) 1 153 2794
Contact: Mr Imre Gyöngyösi
  – Head of Department

ITD Hungary
(Investment and Trade
  Promotion Company,
  owned by MIER)
1051 Budapest
Dorottya u. 4.
Tel: 010 (36) 1 1186 064
Fax: 010 (36) 1 1183 732

Állami Vagyonügynökség (ÁVU)
(State Property Agency)
1133 Budapest
Pozsonyi út. 56.
Tel: 010 (36) 1 129 4800 or
  010 (36) 1 129 4650
Fax: 010 (36) 1 140 2723
Responsible for privatisation
  of state-owned companies.

Állami Vagyonkezelö Rt (ÁV Rt)
(Hungarian State Asset
  Holding Co Ltd)
1115 Budapest
Bánk bán u. 17/B.
Tel: 010 (36) 1 267 6646
Fax: 010 (36) 1 267 6647
Responsible for companies in
  which the state will
  maintain a significant
  shareholding.

HUNGEXPO
Budapest X.
Albertirsai út 10.
Letters: H-1441 Budapest
  POB 44
Tel: 010 (36) 1 263 6000
Fax: 010 (36) 1 263 6098
Responsible for: National
  Trade Fairground and
  organisation of fairs.

MIT-ECONEWS
1016 Budapest
Naphegy tér 8.
Letters: PO Box 3,
  Budapest, H-1426
Tel/fax: 010 (36) 1 118 8204
Telex: 22 4373

Publishes daily economic news summary.

Hungarian Franchise Association
(Magyar Franchise Szövetség)
1097 Budapest
Gyáli út 3/6.
Tel: 010 (36) 1 267 1041
Fax: 010 (36) 1 113 4645
Contact: Mr Endre Fazekas (President)
Executive Director
McDonald's Hungary
Government ministries

Földmüvelésügyi Minisztérium
(Ministry of Agriculture)
1055 Budapest
Kossuth Lajos tér 11.
Tel: 010 (36) 1 153 3000
Fax: 010 (36) 1 153 0518

Müvelödési és Közoktatási Minisztérium
(Ministry of Culture and Education)
1055 Budapest
Szalay u. 10–14.
Tel: 010 (36) 1 153 0600

Honvédelmi Minisztérium
(Ministry of Defence)
1055 Budapest
Balaton u. 7–10
Tel: 010 (36) 1 132 2500

Környezetvédelmi és Területfejlesztési Minisztérium
(Ministry of Environmental

Protection and Regional Development)
1027 Budapest
Fö u. 44–50.
Tel: 010 (36) 1 118 2066

Külügyminisztérium
(Ministry of Foreign Affairs)
1027 Budapest
Bem rkp. 47.
Tel: 010 (36) 1 156 8000

Ipari és Kereskedelmi Minisztérium
(Ministry of Industry & Trade)
1024 Budapest
Margit krt. 85.
Tel: 010 (36) 1 156 5566
Fax: 010 (36) 1 175 0219

Munkaügyi Minisztérium
(Ministry of Labour)
1051 Budapest
Roosevelt tér 7–8.
Tel: 010 (36) 1 132 2100

Közlekedési, Hirközlési és Vizügyi Minisztérium
(Ministry of Transport, Telecommunications and Water Management)
1077 Budapest
Dob u. 77/81
Tel: 010 (36) 1 122 0220

Belügyminisztérium
(Ministry of the Interior)
1051 Budapest
József Attila u. 2–4.
Tel: 010 (36) 1 112 1710

Népjóléti Minisztérium
(Ministry of Welfare)
1051 Budapest
Arany János u. 6–8.
Tel: 010 (36) 1 132 3100

Other government organisations

**MAGYAR NEMZETI
BANK (MNB)**
(National Bank of Hungary)
1054 Budapest V.
Szabadság tér 8/9.
Tel: 010 (36) 1 153 2600,
269 4760
Fax: 010 (36) 1 132 3913
Tlx: 225677

APEH
Adó- és Pénzügyi Ellenörzési
Hivatal
(APEH – Tax and Finance
Controlling Office)
1054 Budapest
Széchenyi u. 2.
Letters: H-1373 Budapest,
Pf. 561.
Tel: 010 (36) 1 112 1890,
112 9620, or
010 (36) 1 112 1990,
111 2219
Fax: 010 (36) 1 153 1853

**KERMI – Kereskedelmi
Minöségellenörzö
Intézet**
(KERMI – Commercial
Quality Control Institute)
1085 Budapest
József krt. 6/8.
Tel: 010 (36) 1 210 0370
Fax: 010 (36) 1 114 3820

**Központi Statisztikai
Hivatal**
(Central Statistical Office)
1024 Budapest
Keleti Károly u. 5–7.
Tel: 010 (36) 1 115 9843

Cégbíróság
(Court of Company
Registration)
1051 Budapest
Nádor u. 28.
Tel: 010 (36) 1 131 1150

**Vám- és Pénzügyörség
Országos
Parancsnokság**
(National HQ of the
Customs and Finance
Guard)
1095 Budapest
Mester u. 7.
Tel: 010 (36) 1 269 9220

KEOK
(Office of Foreigners' Affairs)
1061 Budapest
Andrássy út 12.
Tel: 010 (36) 1 118 3456
Responsible for residence
permits for foreigners.

**Budapesti Munkaügyi
Központ**
(Budapest Labour Centre)
1091 Budapest
Üllöi út 47.
Tel: 010 (36) 1 133 8989
Responsible for work permits
for foreigners.

Market research and credit information

Kopint-Datorg
1051 Budapest
Dorottya u. 6.
Tel: 010 (36) 1 266 6640
Fax: 010 (36) 1 266 6483
Supply market research and business information.

Szonda Ipsos
Média-, Vélemény- és Piackutató Intézet
(Media, Opinion and Market Research Institute)
1081 Budapest
Köztársaság tér 3.
Tel: 010 (36) 1 210 0150
Fax: 010 (36) 1 210 0148

Dun & Bradstreet Hungária Kft
1051 Budapest
Dorottya u. 4.
Tel: 010 (36) 1 118 1997, 118 5044 ext. 252
Fax: 010 (36) 1 118 4985
Tlx: 22 5191

ECONOMIC ASSISTANCE

Ministry of International Economic Relations
H-1055 Budapest
Honved Utca 13–15
Tel: 010 (36) 1 153 2394
Fax: 010 (36) 1 153 0895
Contact: I Gyurkovics, Director General

PHARE Information Office
AN 88 1/26
EC Commission
200 rue de la Loi
B-1049 Brussels
Tel: 010 (32) 2 299 1356/010 (32) 2 299 1400
Fax: 010 (32) 2 299 1777

Know-How Fund
Joint Assistance Unit
Foreign and Commonwealth Office
Old Admiralty Building
London SW1A 2AF
Tel: 44 (71) 210 0023
Fax: 44 (71) 210 0010
Contact: Julian Ebsworth

Joint Industrial and Commercial Attachments Programme
Industrial Training Unit
The British Council
10 Spring Gardens
London SW1A 2BN
Tel: 44 (71) 389 4074
Fax: 44 (71) 839 6347
Contact: Geoff Lincoln

World Bank
Suba Trade Centre
1065 Budapest
Nagymeso Utca 44
Tel: 010 (36) 1 269 0389
Fax: 010 (36) 1 269 0386
Contact: Andrew Rogerson

International Finance Corporation
Suba Trade Centre
1065 Budapest
Nagymeso Utca 44
Tel: 010 (36) 1 269 0384
Fax: 010 (36) 1 269 0388
Contact: Hugh Stevenson

European Bank for Reconstruction and Development
One Exchange Square
London EC2A 2EH

Tel: 44 (71) 338 6000
Fax: 44 (71) 338 6100
Contacts: Gyuri Karady
or
Peter Reiniger, Team
Leaders, Hungary

Paul Dax
Resident Representative
H-1053 Budapest
Kecskemeti utca 7
Tel: 010 (36) 1 266 6000
Fax: 010 (36) 1 266 6003

Index